From C

Managing Change and Transition

Pamela Fleming

© Copyright 2024 - All rights reserved.

The contents of this book may not be reproduced, duplicated, or transmitted without the direct written permission of the author or publisher.

Under no circumstances will the publisher or author be held liable for any damages, recovery, or financial loss due to the information contained in this book. Neither directly nor indirectly.

Table of Contents

Introduction
My Story: A Journey Through Change and Transition 5

Preface
Harness the Power of Effective Change Management, and Transition from Chaos to Clarity with Ease 9

Chapter 1
Setting the Stage - The Mourning After: Navigating Grief in Organizational Change 12

Chapter 2
The Heart of Change: Embracing Emotional Dynamics 20

Chapter 3
Pivoting with Purpose: Understanding Change vs. Transition 25

Chapter 4
The Personal Pace: Supporting Diverse Adaptation Needs 36

Chapter 5
The Insightful Resistance: Learning from Pushback 44

Chapter 6
Transparency in Turbulence: Communicating Through Change ... 55

Chapter 7
Leading with Empathy: The Role of Emotional Intelligence 63

Chapter 8
Roadmap to Change: Orchestrating Change with the Navi5ate Change Framework 75

Chapter 9
Aligning the Alliance: Stakeholder Engagement Strategies 95

Chapter 10
Decisions by Data: Empowering Change with Analytics 104

Chapter 11
Crafting the Core: Building Resilience and Adaptability 109

Chapter 12
Celebrating Small Wins: The Power of Acknowledging Milestones
.... 115

Tying It All Together 124

References 141

INTRODUCTION

My Story: A Journey Through Change and Transition

The Playground Revelation

The playground was alive with the sounds of childhood joy. The merry-go-round spun in a blur of colors, children's laughter filled the air, and the sun cast a warm glow over everything. It was a perfect day, or so it seemed. Amidst the fun, a disagreement broke out, as they often do among children. But this one was different. It ended with words that would change my life forever.

"That's why your mom is not your mom. You are adopted."

The world slowed to a crawl. The merry-go-round seemed to stop mid-spin, the laughter faded, and all I could hear were those words echoing in my mind. I was ten years old, and at that moment, my life as I knew it came to a screeching halt.

I felt a rush of emotions—embarrassment, confusion, and a deep, aching hurt. I ran home with tears streaming down my face and confronted my mom.

"Mom, is it true? Am I adopted?" I asked, my voice trembling.

She looked at me, her eyes filled with hesitation. "Who told you that?" she replied with a stern voice.

"It doesn't matter. Is it true?" I demanded, my heart pounding in my chest.

She sighed deeply. "Yes, you are adopted," she admitted. "Now go play."

That was it, the truth was shrouded in a fog that I could not penetrate. My questions hung in the air, unanswered, and the hurt festered inside me.

The Strain on Family Bonds

For eleven years, I carried that pain with me. It was a heavy burden, a constant reminder of the day my world was turned upside down. The shame and confusion gnawed at me, shaping my teenage years, and casting a shadow over my relationships and self-esteem.

At home, the atmosphere grew tense. My relationship with my mom became strained. Every conversation felt like I was walking on eggshells. My dad tried to bridge the gap, but even his efforts seemed futile. The tension seeped into every corner of our home, creating an invisible barrier that none of us knew how to break.

The Military and the Path to Resolution

Later, joining the military was my escape, a way to find structure and purpose. But it was also where I finally confronted the internal turmoil that had been simmering for over a decade. The discipline and camaraderie of military life forced me to face my past. I realized that if I did not resolve the pain and confusion from my childhood, I would be on a self-destructive path forever asking, "Why me?"

One evening, during a quiet moment in the barracks, I confided in my bunkmate, Jackie.

"Jackie, there's something I've been carrying for a long time," I began, my voice shaky. She looked at me with concern. "What's up? You can tell me anything."

"I found out I was adopted when I was ten. It was a shock, and I've never really dealt with it," I admitted, feeling a weight lift off my shoulders just by saying it out loud.

Jackie nodded, her expression serious. "That's heavy. But you know what? You're not alone. We are all here for you. Maybe it's time to face it head-on."

Through the support of my fellow soldiers and the guidance of mentors, I began to unpack the layers of hurt. I learned to accept my story, to see my adoption not as a source of shame but as a part of who I am. The military gave me the strength and resilience to confront my past and find peace.

A Mission Born from Pain

As I healed, I realized that my experience was not just a personal journey, but a calling. The pain and embarrassment I experienced became the foundation of my life's mission: to ensure that no one transitioning through change feels the way I did. I wanted to help others navigate their own transitions with support and understanding.

Change management became my passion. I saw how effective strategies could ease the process of change, whether in personal lives or within organizations. I dedicated myself to learning everything I could about change management, and the change and transition process, and the psychological effects of change. I wanted to be the guide that I never had, to provide the answers and support that were missing in my own journey.

Through my work, I strive to create environments where people feel safe and supported during times of change. I believe that with the right guidance, change can be a positive and empowering experience. My mission is to turn the pain of my past into a source of strength for others, helping them to navigate their own paths with confidence and resilience.

This is my story—a journey that began with a playground revelation and led to a path of self-discovery and acceptance. It is a tale of hurt and healing, finding strength in vulnerability, and transforming a painful truth into a source of empowerment and purpose. Now you understand the conviction behind my 'WHY'.

From Personal Mission to Professional Passion

As I embraced my mission to help others navigate change, I realized that my personal journey was just the beginning. The lessons I learned from my own experiences became the foundation for a broader understanding of change management. I saw how the principles of managing change could be applied not only to personal transitions but also to organizational and societal shifts.

This realization led me to delve deeper into the field of change management. I pursued formal education and training, learning from experts and gaining certifications. I immersed myself in the study of change theories, models, and best practices. My goal was to equip myself with the knowledge and tools needed to guide others through their own transitions, whether they were individuals, teams, or entire organizations.

In the chapters that follow, I will share the insights and strategies that have shaped my approach to change management. Drawing from both my personal experiences and professional expertise, this book aims to provide a comprehensive guide to navigating change with clarity.

We will explore the core principles of my proprietary Navi5ate (Navigate) Change Framework, focusing on how to prepare for change, engage stakeholders, and sustain momentum. This framework provides practical tools and techniques for managing transitions, including effective communication strategies and comprehensive training programs. Each chapter offers actionable advice and real-world examples to help you apply these concepts within your own context.

Whether you are navigating a personal transition, leading a team through change, or driving organizational transformation, this book is designed to support you every step of the way.

Join me on this journey as we delve into the art and science of managing change and transition.

PREFACE

Harness the Power of Effective Change Management, and Transition from Chaos to Clarity with Ease

"The only thing that is constant is change." - Heraclitus

Change, often perceived as daunting and unwieldy, holds the transformative power to elevate organizational success and resilience. This essence of continuous transformation is the core of "From Chaos to Clarity: Mastering Change and Transition." This book is told from a story-telling perspective of experiences across multiple fortune 500 organizations. As we delve into the intricate world of change management, leaders will learn a proprietary structured framework with actionable strategies to transition from chaos to clarity.

The drive to pen this book stemmed from my personal triumph and my extensive career in change management, where I observed and addressed the hurdles organizations face during transformation. My experience with over 50,000 employees across various industries highlighted a common thread—the profound impact of well-orchestrated change on an organization's health and its people's morale. By sharing these insights, I aim to equip you, the reader, with the tools necessary to master the art of change, reducing fear and resistance and enhancing your leadership acumen. Throughout my journey, I encountered numerous leaders who expressed feelings of being overwhelmed by the scale and pace of change. One poignant example was a healthcare executive who struggled to align his team towards a common vision during a critical system overhaul. His challenge was not unique but rather emblematic of the broader struggles faced by many in leadership positions.

These narratives not only inspired this book but also shaped its content to ensure it is deeply relatable and immensely practical. I extend my heartfelt gratitude to the mentors, colleagues, and friends who supported this endeavor. Their diverse perspectives and unwavering support enriched this work greatly. Special thanks to the Change Navigators LLC team, who tirelessly pursue excellence and consistently exceed client expectations. Your unwavering dedication to client satisfaction is truly commendable and greatly appreciated.

Our shared journey toward mastering change is reflected within these pages. Leaders in all sectors will find valuable insights here, addressing the unique challenges and opportunities within their respective rapidly evolving fields.

As you turn these pages, I invite you to engage with each concept, apply the strategies outlined, and transform potential upheavals into opportunities for growth and innovation. Let's embark on this transformative journey together, navigating through the complexities of change to foster environments where creativity and productivity thrive.

As you embark on each chapter, you will be guided through an immersive leadership journey, presenting various scenarios designed to challenge your thinking and enhance your decision-making skills. You will encounter questions to ponder, using insightful reflections, indicated by a light bulb " 💡 ." We encourage you to pause, consider these questions deeply.

At the conclusion of the book, you will find a dedicated journaling section. This space is intended to serve as a cathartic outlet for expressing your innermost thoughts and feelings. Engaging in journaling here will allow you to deeply reflect on yourself, your leadership abilities, and your approach to change-related situations.

By articulating your thoughts and emotions on paper, you can gain clarity, process your experiences, and promote personal growth. This reflective practice not only deepens your understanding of the concepts discussed in the book but also supports your journey toward becoming a more effective and self-aware leader.

CHAPTER 1

Setting the Stage - The Mourning After: Navigating Grief in Organizational Change

When the Office Walls Speak of Change

The morning sun spilled over the horizon, casting long shadows through the large windows of the office where Sarah worked. The air buzzed with the usual sounds—keyboards clacking, phones ringing softly in their cradles—but today, something was different. A subtle tension hung in the air like a thin curtain, almost imperceptible yet undeniably there.

Sarah sat at her desk, her fingers paused above the keyboard. Her mind wandered back to yesterday's announcement that a major restructuring was on its way. She could still hear her manager's voice, firm yet tinged with an undercurrent of uncertainty as he detailed the upcoming changes. They would lose team members, roles would evolve or disappear and nothing would remain quite as it had been. She felt a pang in her chest—a mix of fear and loss—like saying goodbye to an old friend without having had the chance to prepare.

Around her, murmurs filled the gaps between spurts of forced productivity. Her colleague Tom flicked his pen back and forth between his fingers—a habit when anxiety crept up on him. Sarah noticed his furrowed brow and recalled how they had navigated countless projects together, how their desks had always been islands of certainty in a sea of corporate chaos.

She turned her gaze outside where a group of sparrows fluttered around a feeder hanging from an oak tree. The simplicity of their world struck her; their lives were governed by straightforward needs and immediate concerns. Humans, with all their constructs and expectations, weren't afforded such luxuries.

As she watched them dart through the air, light as whispers against the robust breeze, she pondered on their resilience. Change was constant for them too—seasons shifted--resources fluctuated—yet they adapted swiftly without apparent mourning for what was lost.

> Returning to her screen, Sarah typed out an email meant to reassure her team despite her own swirling doubts. Would acknowledging this shared sense of loss help them move forward? Could they find solace in solidarity? Her finger hesitated over "Send." It wasn't just about adapting to new roles or routines—it was about allowing themselves space to grieve what would no longer be.
>
> The day stretched on like a long pause between chapters in a book you hoped would never end but knew it must. Conversations ebbed and flowed around plans and projections; laughter even found its way through cracks in their armor from time to time, as a reminder that all was not lost.
>
> As evening hues painted skyward canvases in strokes of orange and purple, Sarah stood by those large windows once more. The office slowly emptied; echoes of departure hung heavy around empty chairs and dimmed computer screens.
>
> How do we honor our past contributions while embracing an uncertain future? Is there enough room in our hearts for nostalgia amidst ambition?

Understanding Why We Grieve When Work Changes

Change within organizations is constant, yet its emotional impact often remains unrecognized. As leaders, it is essential to understand the psychological environment of your workplace. When your organization experiences change—be it a policy shift, restructuring, or the introduction of new technology—it can trigger a sense of loss among employees. This loss extends beyond just old software or desks; it involves parting with familiar routines, established understandings, and trusted team dynamics.

Understanding how these shifts impact your team's emotional and psychological well-being is crucial. These effects often subtly influence morale, productivity, and workplace harmony. By recognizing and addressing these hidden impacts, you can foster a more resilient organizational culture.

The Unseen Impact of Change

Change as a Process of Loss

Change, whether in personal life or within an organization, often involves letting go of the familiar. This may involve losing established routines, relationships, roles, or even a sense of identity. Recognizing change as a process of loss helps us understand why it can be so challenging. When people face change, they are not just adapting to new circumstances; they are also mourning what they are leaving behind.

Understanding change as a form of loss provides valuable insight into the emotional complexities involved. It highlights why transitions can be so difficult and why people may resist or struggle with new developments. This perspective allows leaders and individuals to approach change with greater empathy and patience, acknowledging the emotional journey that accompanies it.

In an organizational context, it is crucial to recognize that employees are not merely adapting to new policies or technologies; they are also coping with the emotional impact of losing familiar ways of working and interacting. This loss can affect their sense of stability and security, making it essential for leaders to offer support and understanding during these transitions.

By framing change as a process of loss, leaders can develop strategies that address the emotional needs of those affected. This approach fosters a more compassionate and supportive environment, helping individuals navigate the transition more effectively and emerge stronger on the other side.

Resistance to Change

Resistance to change is a common phenomenon in organizations and is often perceived as a hurdle to be overcome. However, understanding that resistance is rooted in loss allows us to approach it with more empathy. Employees resist change not because they are inherently stubborn or unwilling to adapt, but because they are experiencing a form of grief.

Resistance doesn't arise out of nowhere; it typically stems from changes perceived as negative or imposed without adequate preparation or communication. When employees feel that change is being forced upon them without their input or consideration of their needs, it can lead to feelings of helplessness and frustration. This sense of loss and lack of control can intensify their resistance.

By understanding that resistance is a natural reaction to perceived loss, leaders can gain valuable insights into their team's emotional state. This awareness encourages leaders to communicate more effectively, involve employees in the change process, and provide the necessary support throughout the transition. Addressing these emotional responses can reduce resistance and help build a more positive and resilient organizational culture.

The Role of Grief in Organizational Change

Grief plays a significant role in how individuals respond to change. When an organization undergoes a transformation, employees may grieve the loss of their previous roles, the comfort of familiar processes, or the camaraderie of old teams. This grief can impact their performance, morale, and overall well-being. Recognizing and addressing this grief is crucial for successful change management.

When employees face organizational change, they are not just adapting to new structures or technologies; they are also mourning the loss of what was familiar and comfortable. This sense of loss can manifest in various ways, including decreased productivity, lower morale, and increased resistance to new initiatives. Understanding that these reactions are rooted in grief allows leaders to approach change management with greater empathy and effectiveness.

> **Grief is a natural response to the losses incurred during organizational changes.**

To effectively address grief in the workplace, it's essential to cultivate an environment where employees feel their emotions are recognized and respected. Leaders can achieve this by maintaining transparent and consistent communication about changes, actively listening to employees' concerns, and involving them in the transition process. Additionally, offering resources such as counseling services or support groups can provide crucial assistance, helping employees manage their emotions and adapt more smoothly during challenging times.

Viewing Change Through the Lens of Mourning

Viewing change through the lens of mourning can provide profound insights into the emotional journey that individuals experience during transitions. Just as mourning involves grieving the loss of a loved one, organizational change often entails grieving the loss of familiar routines, relationships, and a sense of stability. This perspective acknowledges that change is not merely a logistical or procedural shift but an emotional upheaval that can evoke feelings of sadness, anxiety, and resistance. By recognizing these emotions as a natural part of the change process, leaders can approach transitions with greater empathy and understanding.

Embracing this viewpoint allows leaders to create a more supportive environment where employees feel their emotions are validated. It encourages open communication, where concerns and fears can be expressed without judgment. Leaders can facilitate this by providing clear information about the changes, involving employees in decision-making, and offering resources such as counseling or support groups. By addressing the emotional aspects of change, organizations can help their teams navigate transitions more effectively, fostering resilience and a stronger sense of community. This compassionate approach not only eases the process of change but also strengthens the overall organizational culture.

Supporting the Mourning Process

When addressing mourning in the workplace, the first step is acknowledgment. Validating employees' feelings can be profoundly comforting, akin to putting a hand on a friend's shoulder during a moment of distress. This simple act shows that their emotions are seen and valued.

Consider holding regular meetings where employees can openly share their feelings and concerns about the changes. These forums provide a crucial outlet for emotions, helping employees process their grief and preventing feelings of isolation. Additionally, introducing flexible support structures, such as counseling sessions or peer support groups, can offer a safety net for those struggling with the transition. Training managers to recognize signs of grief and respond appropriately can also make a significant difference in navigating these turbulent times.

An effective analogy is that of repotting a plant. Just as a plant might wilt temporarily when moved to a new pot, employees might momentarily falter as they adjust to new roles or environments. However, with adequate support and care, they will not only recover but also thrive.

> **What if the key to successful change management is treating the mourning process not as an obstacle but as an integral part of the journey?**

As we move forward in this book, we will delve deeper into the dynamics of change management. You will learn about the Navi5ate Change Framework, a strategic guide designed to enable successful change. This framework helps navigate the complexities of change with empathy and support, ensuring your team can adapt and thrive.

While the Navi5ate Change Framework is a valuable tool, remember that many other frameworks are available. Avoid getting overly attached to a specific framework, as it may not be tailored to your organizational circumstances. Our goal is to provide a structured framework that fits the unique needs of your organization, shaping a future designed specifically for you.

The forthcoming chapters will expand on how to harness these insights to manage change more effectively and propel your team toward unprecedented growth and success. The journey ahead is promising and full of potential for transforming challenges into opportunities for enhancement and innovation. Be prepared to transform your approach to change management by integrating empathy, support, and strategic transition processes. The benefits awaiting you include a more resilient team, a healthier organizational culture, and improved outcomes in all facets of your business operations. Embrace this journey with an open mind and a committed heart, ready to lead and inspire at every step of the way.

Welcome to the upcoming chapters, where *your* story begins.

CHAPTER 2

The Heart of Change: Embracing Emotional Dynamics

Can Emotional Intelligence Pave the Way for Smoother Organizational Change?

In the dim light of early morning, Thomas walked through the quiet halls of the company that had been his second home for nearly two decades. The hum of the fluorescent lights overhead filled the air with a soft, persistent buzz, as if whispering secrets about the impending changes that were unsettling everyone in the office.

Thomas was a middle-aged man with deep-set eyes that often sparkled with a mixture of curiosity and concern. Today, those eyes reflected more of the latter. The company was on the brink of a major transformation, aiming to integrate new technologies that promised efficiency but threatened familiar routines. As he walked past closed office doors and vacant desks, his mind wrestled with the task ahead.

He paused by a window overlooking the city awakening below. Sunlight broke over concrete and glass in silent brilliance. His team had been struggling; not just with learning new systems but coping emotionally with the upheaval. They feared losing their grip on tasks they had mastered over the years, and their anxiety filled each meeting with tension and unspoken questions.

Thomas remembered his own unease during past transitions, feeling as if he were standing on constantly shifting ground. Now, as a leader, he knew he had to guide his team through this maze of uncertainty. He considered how recognizing each person's emotional journey could be as important as any technical training they would undertake.

He returned to his desk and sat down heavily in his chair, feeling the cool leather against his skin. He opened a new email draft, pausing to choose his words carefully. This message needed to reassure, to empathize. He wrote about change, not just as a path to greater efficiency, but as an opportunity for personal growth and reassurance that everyone's voice mattered.

Outside his office door, voices began to fill empty spaces as employees arrived. The clatter of keyboards and murmur of early conversations

> seeped through his door, a reminder that life at work goes on even amid uncertainty.
>
> Thomas leaned back and let out a slow breath. Could he foster resilience within his team by addressing not only what they do but also how they feel? Would acknowledging their fears help them move forward more confidently?
>
> As he pondered these questions, there was a gentle knock at his door, a cue that theory was about to meet practice.
>
> **What steps might leaders take to effectively manage both emotional responses and organizational goals during change?**

Unveiling the Emotional Blueprint of Change

Change is constant, yet it remains one of the most challenging endeavors any organization can undertake. At the heart of this challenge lies not just the structural or strategic adjustments, but a deeper, more personal transition occurring within every individual affected by the change.

Understanding the emotional whirlwind caused by change is not just beneficial; it is imperative for leaders who aim to steer their organizations effectively through periods of uncertainty. The emotional responses of employees—from anxiety and fear to excitement and hope—play a critical role in how change processes are perceived and how well they are executed. Recognizing these emotional undercurrents gives leaders a powerful tool: the ability to align organizational goals with personal motivations, thereby transforming potential resistance into robust support.

Emotions are powerful drivers of human behavior and can significantly influence how change is perceived and adopted. Recognizing the emotional responses to change is crucial because these emotions can either propel progress or stall it. For instance, anxiety might cause an employee to resist a new process or procedure, while understanding and acceptance may accelerate adoption.

Consider the analogy of a gardener tending to plants. Just as a gardener must understand the specific needs of each plant to nurture it effectively, leaders must comprehend the diverse emotional states of their team members to guide them through transitions smoothly. This understanding can transform potential resistance into a collaborative effort towards change.

Leaders should not only recognize but also validate these emotional experiences. Validation does not mean agreeing with everyone's emotions but acknowledging their existence and legitimacy. This acknowledgment can alleviate stress and build trust, making employees feel valued and understood.

> Understanding and addressing the emotional dynamics of change is essential for smooth transitions.

Cultivating a Supportive Environment

It is not enough to recognize emotions; effective leaders must also act to support their teams' emotional well-being. This support can take many forms, from open communication channels to personalized training and counseling opportunities. The objective is to create an environment where employees feel secure enough to express and manage their emotions.

An effective way to cultivate this environment is through regular and structured **team meetings** where not only are **updates shared**, but **feedback is solicited** and valued. This practice helps in making the employees feel heard and respected, which can enhance their commitment to the organizational goals.

Training sessions tailored to address changes can alleviate fears by equipping employees with the necessary tools and knowledge. A supportive strategy might be likened to providing a safety net. Just as a trapeze artist is more likely to perform better knowing there is a safety net, employees are likely to engage more positively with change if they know there is support available.

Empathy and **compassion** are vital in this process. Acknowledging the challenges and stresses that come with change allows leaders to approach transitions with a supportive mindset. This approach is crucial because it helps in reducing resistance and fostering a more engaged workforce. When employees feel supported, their trust in the organization increases, enhancing their willingness to embrace new changes.

Collaboration emerges as a powerful tool in managing change effectively. Involving all stakeholders in the decision-making process empowers them while ensuring diverse perspectives are considered, leading to more robust and sustainable change initiatives. This inclusive approach not only smooths the transition process but also bolsters the organization's resilience in the face of future challenges.

As we move forward, the focus will shift from understanding the foundational aspects of emotional dynamics in change to exploring more complex strategies in change management. Each chapter builds on the last, equipping you with a comprehensive toolkit that will transform your approach to leading change.

The journey ahead promises to be insightful, empowering you with the knowledge to anticipate challenges and harness the opportunities that change inevitably brings.

CHAPTER 3

Pivoting with Purpose: Understanding Change vs. Transition

Can a Leader Navigate the Storm of Change and Still Keep the Crew Together?

In the dim light of early morning, Thomas stood by the vast windows of his office, overlooking the steel and glass that made up the city's skyline. The sun, a reluctant riser, cast a pale glow that barely touched the edges of his coffee cup. Today marked the commencement of a major structural overhaul at his company, where he had been at the helm for over five years. The change was necessary, inevitable even, with technology evolving at breakneck speed. But as he sipped his coffee, his mind was not on systems or structures; it dwelled on his team.

Down in the parking lot, he watched as Sarah, one of his longest-serving team members, arrived. Her stride was slower than usual, and her shoulders hunched as if she carried more than just her laptop bag. Last week's meeting replayed in Thomas's mind where he had announced the upcoming changes. He remembered seeing the tight smiles and nodding heads but also noted the anxiety-laden glances exchanged when they thought he was not looking.

Inside his spacious office filled with mementos of past successes—a stark contrast to what lay outside—Thomas paced back and forth on the plush carpet that muffled his steps. Each step was a silent question: How do you prepare people for change? How do you transition not just processes but people? The aroma of coffee mingled with that of aged paper from books lining his shelves, a comforting scent that usually calmed him but today seemed to mock his unease.

Interrupting his contemplation was Julie's knock on the door frame. "Morning Thomas," she greeted him with her usual warmth, tinged today with hesitation. "The team's gathering for your briefing." As they walked down the hallways adorned with abstract art, a stark reminder of change being both complex and colorful, Thomas felt every eye upon him as if they were trying to decipher what lay behind his composed facade.

In these moments walking towards what could be an uncomfortable assembly, Thomas realized this was more than just guiding them through a transition; it was about leading by understanding their fears

> and aspirations. It was not enough to implement new software or streamline operations if those driving these very changes felt left behind.
>
> As they reached their destination, the conference room was bustling with low murmurs—he paused at the door. Would this meeting be another series of nods and smiles masking true feelings? Or would it be where they started to truly navigate this transition together?

Is Your Leadership Ready for the True Challenge of Change?

When organizations undertake change initiatives, leaders typically focus on external factors such as new technologies, updated strategies, and revised structures. However, the internal dynamics—how employees perceive and adapt to these changes—are often neglected. Yet, these internal processes are equally important, if not more so. Understanding the critical difference between change and transition is essential for any leader seeking successful transformation.

Mastering this distinction enables leaders to navigate the complexities of organizational shifts more effectively. By recognizing that change involves external adjustments while transition pertains to the internal process of adapting, leaders can better support their teams through uncertainty, foster resilience, and drive meaningful progress. This insight is key to ensuring that transformations are not just implemented but embraced by all.

Change is often described as a journey filled with twists and turns, and indeed, it is. Yet, it is the transition through this change that frequently leads to misalignment on the people side. Change itself is relatively straightforward—it encompasses the tangible shifts within an organization, such as new policies, software systems, or team structures. These changes are visible and quantifiable.

Transition, however, is far more intricate. It delves into the internal processes that individuals experience as they navigate change. This psychological journey involves adjusting to new ways of working and thinking, and it is here that leaders must tread carefully. While they can enforce change, transitions are organic and require empathy and support. Ignoring the nuances of internal transitions can result in resistance, diminished morale, and a failure to integrate new practices sustainably.

Physical changes are easily observed and measured, but the psychological transitions often present greater challenges. Employees face a range of emotions—anxiety, confusion, excitement, and hope—as they grapple with uncertainty and strive to build new habits. Understanding this emotional landscape is crucial. By identifying signs of discomfort or resistance early on, leaders can respond proactively, providing the support necessary to ease the transition. This not only smooths the process but also cultivates a culture of trust and resilience within the organization.

Moreover, it's essential to evaluate the effectiveness of managing transitions—not just by project success rates but also by measuring employee satisfaction and retention during significant changes. Robust metrics and feedback systems are vital for gauging how well an organization navigates these challenging periods. By mastering the distinction between change and transition, leaders can ensure a more holistic approach to transformation, ultimately leading to lasting success.

Understanding the Difference: Change vs. Transition

Mastering the distinction between the Big "C" and the little "c" is essential for effective leadership in times of transformation. The Big "C" signifies major, transformative changes that fundamentally reshape entire systems or organizations—think company-wide restructurings or sweeping technological upgrades. In contrast, the little "c" encompasses not only non-transformational shifts and simple transitions but also emphasizes the people-side of change. It represents the vital efforts change leaders make to support and guide individuals through the intricate journey from their current reality to a desired future.

Both dimensions of change are indispensable, yet they demand a nuanced approach to recognize and manage their distinct impacts.

Change, as represented by the Big "C," is an external event. It refers to tangible shifts—the new system implementation, organizational redesign, or office relocation. These changes disrupt the status quo and are often propelled by external factors like technological advancements, market dynamics, and socio-political shifts. To navigate this complex landscape effectively, leaders must not only focus on the mechanics of change but also prioritize the emotional and psychological transitions of their teams. Let's look at some examples of Big "C" transformations.

For instance, **technological innovations** like the adoption of artificial intelligence or new software systems can necessitate a move to a new system. **Market fluctuations**, such as economic downturns or shifts in consumer preferences, might prompt an organizational redesign to stay competitive. And **socio-political changes**, including new regulations or evolving social values, can lead to changes like an office move to comply with new standards or to better align with societal expectations.

Imagine Big "C" change as the act of moving to a new house. The physical act of transporting belongings from one place to another is visible and often swift. However, settling into a new neighborhood, making it feel like home, is a personal journey requiring time and adaptation. This is where the concept of transition, the little "c" comes into play.

Transition is less about the logistical aspects and more about the human side of change. Think of it as the incremental shifts that take place. While change refers to the external events or situations that alter our circumstances, transition is the internal process that individuals go through as they adapt to these changes. It involves a series of psychological adjustments that are crucial for embracing new realities.

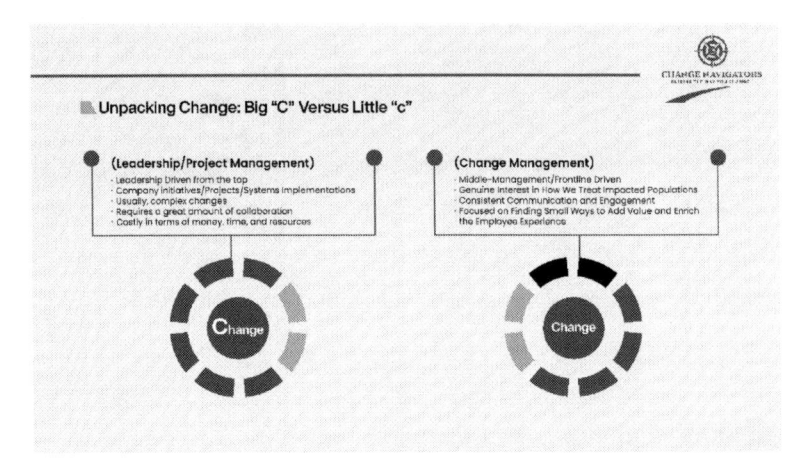

Figure 1: Pamela R. Fleming, (2024) Big "C" versus Little "c." Change Navigators LLC.

Recognizing the Importance of Internal Transitions

When change is announced, the first reactions are often shock and denial, which are natural parts of the transition process. Understanding this, leaders must create an environment where employees feel supported throughout their personal transitions. This support is crucial because it affects how quickly and effectively team members can move through their own internal processes to embrace the new changes.

Imagine a butterfly emerging from its chrysalis. The process of transformation is both beautiful and challenging. Initially, the butterfly struggles to unfold its wings, and it may appear vulnerable as it adjusts to its new form. This delicate stage mirrors the experience of an employee navigating change within an organization.

Just as the butterfly requires time to strengthen its wings and gain confidence in its ability to fly, employees need support and encouragement to adapt to new roles, processes, or environments. With the right guidance, resources, and nurturing, they will eventually soar, embracing their new capabilities and contributing to the organization's growth.

Addressing the internal transitions of employees is not just about being considerate; it is a strategic action that directly impacts the success of the organizational changes. Employees who feel understood and supported are more likely to engage with new initiatives and drive better results.

> 💡 Could the difference between a successful change and a failed one be as simple as ensuring that employees feel supported in their transitions?

Leaders should employ empathy, actively listen to employee concerns, and provide clear, continuous communication. Let's explore some key elements of transition. These actions help employees navigate their internal transitions, reducing resistance and fostering a more adaptable and resilient workforce.

Elements of Transition

Feelings:

Emotional Responses: Transition often triggers a range of emotions, from excitement and anticipation to anxiety and grief. These feelings are natural as individuals navigate the uncertainty and ambiguity that comes with change.

Emotional Support: Providing emotional support and acknowledging these feelings can help individuals cope better with the transition process.

Expectations:

Managing Expectations: Transition involves adjusting expectations to align with the new situation. This can mean letting go of old expectations and forming new ones that are realistic and achievable.

Communication: Clear and open communication about what to expect can ease the transition and reduce anxiety.

Mental Adjustments:

Cognitive Shifts: Transition requires a shift in mindset. This might involve rethinking old habits, beliefs, and attitudes to fit the new context.

Learning and Adaptation: Embracing change often means acquiring new skills and knowledge. This learning process is a critical part of mental adjustments during transition.

The Process of Transition

The Process of Transition is a multifaceted journey that can be segmented into three core stages. Each stage plays a crucial role in facilitating a smooth and effective change, ensuring that individuals and organizations can adapt and thrive in new environments. By understanding and navigating these stages, one can better manage the challenges and opportunities that come with any significant transition.

Letting Go: Embrace the inevitability of change. This stage is often met with resistance and requires intentional, targeted communication and engagement efforts.

This stage involves acknowledging and accepting the end of the old ways. It can be a time of loss and grief as individuals let go of familiar routines and identities.

The Messy Middle: Navigate the transitional phase, which can vary in duration and is deeply personal.

This period is characterized by ambiguity and uncertainty. While the old ways have ended, the new ones are not yet fully established. It can be uncomfortable, but also offers opportunity for creativity and exploration.

The New Horizon: Cultivate and sustain the new state while being mindful of potential setbacks to the messy middle if the little "c" is not acknowledged.

In this stage, individuals begin to embrace the new reality. They form new identities, adopt new behaviors, and establish new ways of working and living. This phase is marked by a renewed sense of purpose and energy.

Implementing Support Mechanisms

To drive successful transitions, organizations must establish robust support mechanisms that prioritize the emotional and psychological well-being of their employees. This encompasses dynamic training programs, impactful mentorship, regular feedback sessions, and open forums for candid discussion. These initiatives empower employees to grasp the nuances of change, clarify their roles in the evolving landscape, and articulate their concerns and suggestions. By fostering an environment of support and open communication, organizations can inspire resilience and engagement, ensuring that every team member feels valued and equipped to thrive.

Consider the analogy of a guide helping a traveler navigate a new city. The guide provides insights, points out hazards, and highlights opportunities, making the journey less daunting and more enjoyable. In the same way, support mechanisms in an organization guide employees through new territories of practice and policy, boosting their confidence and competence.

Support mechanisms are not just about easing the transition but are essential tools that empower employees to embrace and excel in the new environment created by change.

> **By differentiating between change and transition, leaders can ensure their organizations are creating an adaptable workforce primed for future challenges.**

Implementing support mechanisms plays a pivotal role in this process. These mechanisms should be designed to assist employees in understanding, accepting, and embracing the changes. Whether through training sessions, workshops, continuous communication, or strategic employee engagements, these resources help bridge the gap between the old and the new, ensuring that employees feel valued and supported throughout the transition.

Supporting Transition

To support individuals through transition, it is important to:

Acknowledge the Emotional Impact: Recognize and validate the emotions that come with change.

Provide Clear Information: Offer clear and consistent information about what is changing and why.

Encourage Open Communication: Create a safe space for individuals to express their concerns and ask questions.

Offer Resources and Support: Provide access to resources such as counseling, training, and peer support groups.

Be Patient and Compassionate: Understand that transition takes time, and everyone moves through it at their own pace.

By embedding these practices into the core of change management, organizations can achieve far more than mere operational success; they can foster a culture of inclusivity and understanding that honors the contributions and well-being of every team member. This rich environment not only propels performance but also fortifies organizational resilience and enhances return on investment.

Embracing a dual focus on both change and transition equips leaders with vital tools to navigate the complexities of organizational transformation. It highlights the essential nature of partnership and collaboration in reaching shared objectives, while also illuminating the transformative power of empathetic leadership in driving successful change initiatives.

While a leader can mandate change overnight, the journey of transition is far more intricate and time-consuming. It requires individuals to internally adjust to their new reality, taking the necessary time to comprehend, accept, and find their place within the new framework.

In their haste to implement change, leaders often overlook the critical necessity of this transition. They may fixate on metrics of success and milestone completion, neglecting the foundational role that the human experience plays in these processes. Without addressing the emotional and psychological dimensions of change, even the most meticulously crafted plans can unravel. This is why the little "c" must be recognized as a pivotal factor in fostering awareness and promoting genuine adoption.

> **Change is what happens *to* people, transition is what happens *inside* people.**

CHAPTER 4

The Personal Pace: Supporting Diverse Adaptation Needs

How Does One Navigate the Headwinds of Change?

Julia sat by the window, her gaze fixed on the restless leaves dancing to the tune of the autumn wind. The office was quiet today-quieter than usual. Her colleagues, scattered like chess pieces across the room, seemed absorbed in their tasks. Today marked a year since she had stepped into the role of a manager, a position that carried the weighty responsibility of guiding her team through an impending corporate restructuring.

Her fingers tapped a nervous rhythm on her desk, mirroring her inner disquiet. Julia remembered her own struggle with change and how it felt like swimming against a relentless tide. Her thoughts shifted to Tom, who had just returned from paternity leave and already seemed overwhelmed with minor adjustments at work. Then there was Elsie, usually so composed, who confessed just last week that she feared what these changes might mean for her position.

A soft murmur pulled Julia from her thoughts. Across from her, Tom fumbled with his new software update. She watched as his brow furrowed in concentration and frustration. It was clear he needed support but not the kind that was currently available.

Julia stood and walked over to him, her steps slow and deliberate on the soft carpet. "How's it going with the update?" she asked.

"It's... different," Tom replied hesitantly. "I'm trying to get used to it."

Her heart sank a little at his understated distress; change was never easy. Julia suggested they schedule regular check-ins-- not just for project updates but also to share concerns about these transitions. As she spoke, she noticed Elsie looking over with a faint smile of gratitude.

Returning to her desk, Julia glanced outside once more where the wind continued its playful havoc among the trees—a silent reminder that change is constant, but its reception need not be harsh or cold.

> She mulled over creating diverse support systems tailored not just for adapting to new software or protocols but also for managing the emotional landscapes that such changes invariably sculpted within each individual.
>
> Could understanding and addressing personal responses to change make all the difference?

One Size Does Not Fit All: Tailoring Change Management to Individual Needs

In the realm of organizational change, recognizing that each team member adapts at their own pace is not just beneficial—it is essential. Understanding the personal rhythms of adaptation significantly influences the effectiveness of change management. Leaders must embrace these differences to cultivate a supportive and resilient workplace.

First, it's vital to acknowledge the diverse paces at which team members adjust to change. These differences often stem from unique personal experiences, temperaments, and external circumstances beyond the workplace. By identifying these variations early, leaders can anticipate challenges and address them proactively, setting the stage for smoother transitions.

Next, organizations must design and implement supportive mechanisms that respect and enhance this diversity within the workforce. This means creating a range of resources and support systems that are accessible to everyone but can be customized to meet individual needs. Such mechanisms not only make employees feel valued and understood but also foster a more inclusive organizational culture.

Moreover, enhancing team resilience emerges as a critical outcome of providing tailored support strategies. These strategies should consider both personal and professional challenges that employees encounter during transitions. By addressing these needs, organizations can transform potential resistance into lasting resilience, empowering employees to thrive amid change.

Empathetic leadership is pivotal in this process. By stepping into team members' shoes, leaders can gain a deeper understanding of their perspectives and emotional responses to change. This insight enables the crafting of interventions that resonate profoundly with employees.

A strategy that accounts for individual adaptation speeds and personal circumstances ensures that initiatives are as effective as possible. This approach not only improves organizational outcomes but also elevates employee well-being and job satisfaction.

Through strategic empathy and tailored support, leaders can enhance both individual and organizational resilience, turning potential disruptions into opportunities for growth and development. The path forward is clear.

Understanding Team Adaptation Paces

When managing change, it's vital to recognize that team members will navigate transitions at their own unique paces. Picture a diverse forest, where each tree grows at a different rate, influenced by its surroundings. Just as some trees flourish in sunlight while others thrive in shade, employees adapt to change in distinct ways. Some may eagerly tackle new challenges, while others might require more time to find their footing.

This variation in adaptation speeds can be shaped by numerous factors, including personal backgrounds, past experiences, and current life circumstances. For instance, a seasoned employee may quickly embrace new processes, drawing on their wealth of knowledge, while a newcomer might need extra training and support to build confidence. Additionally, personal circumstances—such as caregiving responsibilities or health concerns—can significantly affect how swiftly someone can adjust to workplace changes.

By understanding these nuances, leaders can cultivate a nurturing environment that empowers all team members to flourish, ensuring that no one is left behind in the transition.

Metaphor: The Marathon Runner

Imagine change as a marathon, not a sprint. In this race, every runner has a unique rhythm—some burst out of the gate with speed and enthusiasm, while others conserve their energy, pacing themselves for the long journey ahead. This metaphor captures how employees navigate change within the workplace.

Some team members may swiftly embrace new processes or systems, charging forward with eagerness and passion. They thrive on the thrill of new challenges, ready to implement changes without hesitation. In contrast, others adopt a more deliberate approach, taking the time to fully understand and accept the new landscape before diving in. This careful pacing allows them to establish a solid foundation and ensure they are comfortable with the changes.

Recognizing these differing paces is crucial for effective change management. Just as a marathon coach tailors training plans to fit each runner's strengths and needs, leaders must provide personalized support and resources to help every team member adapt at their own speed. This strategy not only respects individual differences but also fosters a more inclusive and supportive work environment, enabling everyone to thrive in the race of change.

Tailoring Support

Leaders must be attuned to the diverse needs of their team members and be prepared to offer tailored levels of support. Just as a tailor customizes a suit to fit an individual's unique measurements, leaders should tailor their support to fit the unique needs of each employee. This might involve providing additional training sessions for those who need more time to adapt to new changes. For employees who thrive under direct guidance, more frequent check-ins and one-on-one meetings can be beneficial.

Recognizing and accommodating these varying paces is crucial for fostering an inclusive and supportive workplace environment. By offering personalized support, leaders can ensure that all team members feel valued and understood, leading to a more cohesive and productive team. This approach not only helps individuals succeed but also strengthens the overall team dynamic, making it more resilient in the face of change.

Fact-Based Support Systems

Envision a support system rooted in facts, meticulously designed to address the diverse needs of your team. For many employees, mentorship programs offer the perfect space to flourish—providing personalized guidance from seasoned colleagues at their own pace. This tailored approach cultivates confidence and competence, allowing growth to unfold gradually and meaningfully.

On the other hand, some employees thrive in group training sessions that create a vibrant sense of community and collective learning. These collaborative environments encourage team members to share insights and support one another throughout the transition. The shared experience fosters motivation and reassurance, making each individual feel more connected and empowered in their learning journey.

By embracing both individualized mentorship and group training, organizations can create a dynamic support system that meets every team member where they are, driving both personal and collective success.

Rhetorical Consideration: What If?

What if every organization could tailor its support mechanisms to meet the unique needs of each employee? The potential surge in employee satisfaction and productivity could transform our entire perception of work. Imagining this possibility can ignite a spark in leaders to innovate and adopt more personalized approaches to employee support, reshaping the future of work for the better.

The Tailored Transition Process

The **Tailored Transition Process** is designed to assess, categorize, implement, and evaluate personalized support strategies within an organization. This ensures that each team member receives the appropriate resources and support to adapt effectively to changes. The goal is to develop a resilient workforce capable of thriving through change by providing personalized support that acknowledges individual adaptation needs. Here are considerations when tailoring your specific transition:

- **Assess Individual Needs**
  Start by conducting thorough assessments such as surveys, interviews, or focus groups to understand each team member's unique challenges and preferences regarding change. Timeframe: 1-2 weeks.

- **Categorize Adaptation Needs**
  Based on the collected data, group these needs into measurable categories. This helps in tailoring specific support mechanisms such as additional training or mentorship programs. Timeframe: 1 week.

- **Implement Support Structures**
  Launch the support mechanisms and communicate them effectively through emails, intranet postings and meetings to ensure accessibility. Timeframe: 2-3 weeks.

- **Maintain Open Communication**
  Foster open communication by encouraging regular concerns and feedback. This step is crucial for adjusting support strategies as needed. Timeframe: Ongoing.

- **Foster a Safe Emotional Environment**
  Create platforms such as forums or feedback sessions where employees can share their feelings and experiences related to the change. Timeframe: Ongoing.
- **Evaluate and Adjust**
  Regularly assess the effectiveness of support structures through feedback and make necessary adjustments; ensuring strategies remain effective and relevant. Timeframe: Every 3-6 months.

By implementing the Tailored Transition Process, leaders can ensure that each team member feels valued and supported through changes, leading to a more adaptable and resilient organization. This approach bolsters individual well-being and collective strength, paving the way for successful organizational transformations. Empathetic leadership and strategic support can transform potential resistance into resilience, fostering an environment where both individuals and the organization can thrive amidst change.

To ensure this process resonates with your organization's vision and mission, give your tailored process a name, meaning consider gamification with a naming contest. This is also a good way to drive awareness and engagement amongst employees.

CHAPTER 5

The Insightful Resistance: Learning from Pushback

Can Resistance Illuminate the Path to Harmony?

In the dim light of early morning, Thomas walked through the quiet halls of the manufacturing plant he managed. The hum of machinery was still silent, an unusual peace before the storm of activity that would soon ensue. He could feel the weight of impending changes hanging over him like thick fog over a harbor.

Thomas had announced a major operational shift —a move towards automation that promised efficiency but threatened the traditional way his team worked. The backlash was immediate; faces etched with concern and voices tinged with bitterness filled his office all day. He understood their fears-- change was an intruder that came uninvited, demanding adaptation when comfort felt much sweeter.

As he passed by the assembly line, he paused to run his hand over a cold, metallic arm of what would soon replace some of these functions. The steel didn't warm under his touch, nor did it return any sense of loyalty or years of service like his employees did. He remembered Mark's words from yesterday, "We aren't just cogs in your machine, Thomas." That sentence echoed in his mind, bouncing off the walls built from years of shared successes and struggles.

Outside, a light drizzle began to tap on the factory windows—a soft but persistent reminder that nature itself adapts continuously. Thomas watched as droplets formed rivulets on glass panes, each taking its own path yet influenced by those around it. Could resistance be like these water droplets? Not just obstacles but guides towards a more natural path?

He thought about how resistance had revealed undercurrents of fear and uncertainty among his staff. It was not just about new technology; it was about respect for their labor and fear for their future relevance. Perhaps this resistance was not something to overcome but to understand and integrate into his plans.

As he turned back towards his office, ready to face another round of discussions and debates, he wondered if this resistance could indeed be channeled into constructive dialogue, transforming discord into a

> symphony where every note mattered.
>
> 💡 **Could listening to employees' chorus of concerns not only ease the transition but improve it beyond what Thomas initially envisioned?**

Embracing Resistance: An Unlikely Catalyst for Change

When leaders embark on the journey of transforming their organizations, resistance is often met with frustration. Yet, what if this resistance is not just a barrier but a beacon guiding us towards a more profound understanding and more effective strategies? By shifting our perspective from combating resistance to learning from it, we can uncover invaluable insights that enhance our approach to managing change.

Resistance in the workplace is frequently viewed as an impediment to progress. However, it is essential to recognize that **resistance often stems from legitimate concerns** and uncertainties among team members. Identifying the underlying causes of this pushback not only addresses immediate issues but also strengthens the organization's adaptive capabilities overall.

Identifying the Roots of Resistance

When teams resist change, their reluctance is often rooted in deeper issues. Like a tree with deep, intertwining roots, this resistance can spring from fears of the unknown or perceived threats to job security. For leaders, grasping these underlying concerns is essential, as abrupt organizational shifts can significantly unsettle team members, especially when they feel disregarded.

To navigate this landscape, leaders must engage openly with their teams. By asking questions and actively listening to concerns, they can uncover specific fears and objections. This dialogue not only reveals the true sources of resistance but also fosters empathy—a vital trait in effective leadership. It emphasizes the importance of recognizing the human element within the organizational framework.

Moreover, resistance can be fueled by a history of mistrust or past initiatives that failed to resonate with the team. Such experiences can cast a long shadow over morale and erode confidence in leadership. By acknowledging these past missteps and demonstrating a commitment to learning from them, leaders can gradually rebuild trust and pave the way for more transparent communication. Through understanding and collaboration, teams can transform resistance into resilience, embracing change as an opportunity for growth.

> **Understanding the roots of resistance involves recognizing and addressing the deeper concerns of team members, fostering an environment of trust and open communication.**

Using Resistance as a Diagnostic Tool

Resistance isn't merely an obstacle; it's a powerful diagnostic tool that uncovers deeper issues within an organization. Every pushback or objection is a clue, revealing what might be lacking or misaligned in your change initiative.

Think of resistance as a symptom, much like a fever that indicates a health problem. Just as a doctor investigates various tests to diagnose the cause of a fever, leaders must delve into resistance to unearth the underlying concerns driving it.

By meticulously mapping when and where resistance surfaces, leaders can identify specific areas in their change plans that need greater focus or revision. This analysis can unveil patterns of resistance linked to particular departments, roles, or specific elements of the change initiative.

Moreover, integrating feedback mechanisms—such as surveys or focus groups—can serve as critical diagnostic tools. These approaches offer structured channels for employees to voice their concerns and for leaders to collect actionable insights.

So, how can we adapt our strategies based on these diagnostic findings? It's not just about alleviating fears; it's about enhancing the effectiveness of the change process. Let's dive deeper into this exploration.

Developing Actionable Strategies for Harnessing Resistance

Crafting strategies to address and leverage resistance constructively is crucial for transforming challenges into valuable opportunities for growth. Resistance, often viewed negatively, can actually serve as a catalyst for improvement when approached thoughtfully.

To effectively harness resistance, it's important to design interventions that not only tackle the root causes of objections but also actively engage employees in the change process. Here are some strategies to consider:

Change Ambassador Program

One effective strategy is to create change ambassador programs. This involves selecting a diverse group of team members to act as change ambassadors, facilitating better communication between leadership and the workforce. Here's how to build this out:

Selection Process: Carefully select ambassadors from various departments, roles, and levels within the organization. Ensure diversity in terms of experience, background, and perspectives to represent the entire workforce effectively. Aim for 1 to 2% of the employee population.

Training and Empowerment: Provide comprehensive training to the ambassadors on the principles of change management, communication skills, and conflict resolution. Equip them with the knowledge and tools they need to effectively support their peers and advocate for the change. Continue to offer optional developmental micro-learning opportunities.

Clear Roles and Responsibilities: Clearly define ambassadors' roles as liaisons between leadership and employees. They should gather and relay feedback, clarify misunderstandings, and promote the benefits of the change initiatives.

Regular Meetings and Updates: Schedule regular meetings with the ambassadors to review progress, challenges, and feedback from their teams. These meetings should be a platform for ambassadors to share insights and for leadership to provide updates and address any concerns.

Communication Channels: Establish dedicated communication channels for ambassadors to connect with their peers and leadership. This could include internal messaging platforms, dedicated email groups, or regular town hall meetings.

Recognition and Support: Recognize and reward the efforts of change ambassadors. Acknowledge their contributions through formal recognition programs, incentives, or career development opportunities. Ensure they have ongoing support from leadership to perform their roles effectively.

Feedback Integration: Encourage ambassadors to continuously gather feedback from their teams and integrate this feedback into the change management process. Address resistance early and align initiatives with employee needs and concerns.

Monitoring and Evaluation: Regularly monitor the effectiveness of the change ambassador program. Evaluate its impact on communication, employee engagement, and the overall success of the change initiatives. Adjust as needed to improve the program's effectiveness.

Comprehensive Feedback Loop System

A more nuanced strategy involves establishing a comprehensive feedback loop system. This system should be designed to continuously gather, analyze, and act on feedback from employees at all levels. Here's how to build this out:

Multi-Channel Feedback Collection: Utilize various channels such as surveys, suggestion boxes, focus groups, and one-on-one meetings to collect feedback. This ensures that all employees, regardless of their communication preferences, have a voice.

Real-Time Feedback Tools: Implement digital tools that allow real-time feedback. Platforms like employee engagement apps can facilitate instant feedback on specific initiatives or general workplace sentiments.

Regular Analysis and Reporting: Establish a routine for analyzing feedback data. Use analytics to identify trends, common concerns, and areas of resistance. Regularly report these findings to leadership and relevant teams to ensure timely action.

Actionable Insights: Translate feedback into actionable insights. Develop specific action plans to address identified issues. This might involve policy changes, additional training, or adjustments to the change management strategy.

Close the Loop: Ensure that employees see the impact of their feedback. Communicate the actions taken in response to their input and the outcomes of those actions. This transparency builds trust and reinforces the value of their contributions.

Continuous Improvement: Treat the feedback loop as an ongoing process rather than a one-time effort. Regularly update the system based on its effectiveness and the evolving needs of the organization.

Implementing a Reward System

Recognizing and rewarding adaptability can significantly motivate employees to embrace change. Implementing a reward system that acknowledges those who demonstrate flexibility and a positive attitude towards change can encourage others to follow suit. Here's how to build this out:

Define Clear Criteria: Establish clear criteria for what constitutes adaptability and a positive attitude towards change. This could include behaviors such as proactive problem-solving, willingness to learn new skills, and supporting colleagues during transitions.

Diverse Reward Mechanisms: Implement a variety of reward mechanisms to cater to different preferences. These can include monetary bonuses, additional paid time off, public recognition, career development opportunities, and personalized rewards that align with individual interests.

Regular Recognition Programs: Create regular recognition programs such as "Employee of the Month" or "Change Champion Awards" to highlight and celebrate those who exemplify adaptability. Ensure these programs are well-publicized and celebrated within the organization.

Peer Recognition: Encourage peer-to-peer recognition where employees can nominate colleagues who have shown exceptional adaptability. This not only broadens the scope of recognition but also fosters a supportive and appreciative work culture.

Feedback and Testimonials: Collect feedback and testimonials from employees who have been recognized for their adaptability. Share their stories and experiences through internal newsletters, meetings, or the company intranet to inspire others and highlight the tangible benefits of embracing change.

Leadership Involvement: Ensure that leadership is actively involved in the recognition process. Leaders should regularly acknowledge and reward adaptability in team meetings, town halls, and other forums. This demonstrates the organization's commitment to valuing adaptability.

Continuous Improvement: Regularly review and update the reward system based on employee feedback and the evolving needs of the organization. Ensure that the system remains relevant, fair, and motivating for all employees.

Link to Career Growth: Connect adaptability recognition to career growth opportunities. Highlight how demonstrating flexibility and a positive attitude towards change can lead to promotions, leadership roles, and other career advancements within the organization.

Training and Development Programs

Micro-learning training and development offerings tailored to change management can equip team members with the necessary skills and knowledge to navigate the transition. These programs should focus on emotional intelligence and building resilience and adaptability, empowering employees to manage changes more confidently. Here's how to build this out:

Bite-Sized Learning Modules: Develop short, focused learning modules that employees can complete in a few minutes. These modules should cover key aspects of change management, such as understanding the change process, managing stress, and developing a growth mindset.

Emotional Intelligence Training: Include specific modules on emotional intelligence (EI). These should cover self-awareness, self-regulation, empathy, and social skills. Practical exercises and scenarios can help employees apply EI principles in real-life situations.

Resilience Building: Create training sessions that focus on building resilience. Topics can include coping strategies, stress management techniques, and ways to maintain a positive outlook during times of change. Interactive activities and reflection exercises can enhance learning.

Adaptability Skills: Offer modules that teach adaptability skills. This can include lessons on flexibility, problem-solving, and innovation. Encourage employees to embrace change as an opportunity for growth and learning.

Interactive and Engaging Content: Use a variety of multimedia content such as videos, infographics, quizzes, and interactive simulations to make the learning experience engaging and effective. Gamification elements like badges and leaderboards can also motivate participation.

On-Demand Access: Ensure that the micro-learning modules are accessible on-demand, allowing employees to learn at their own pace and convenience. Mobile-friendly platforms can facilitate learning anytime, anywhere.

Regular Updates and New Content: Keep the training content fresh and relevant by regularly updating existing modules and adding new ones. This ensures that employees are always equipped with the latest knowledge and skills.

Feedback and Assessment: Incorporate feedback mechanisms and assessments to gauge the effectiveness of the training. Use surveys, quizzes, and performance metrics to identify areas for improvement and to tailor future training offerings.

Supportive Learning Environment: Foster a supportive learning environment by encouraging managers and leaders to participate in the training alongside their teams. This demonstrates a commitment to continuous learning and sets a positive example.

Integration with Broader Change Initiatives: Align the micro-learning offerings with broader change management initiatives. Ensure that the training supports the overall goals of the organization's change strategy and reinforces key messages.

It is also vital to maintain transparency throughout the change process.

Regular updates and open dialogues about the progress and challenges of the initiative help in maintaining trust and managing expectations. This openness allows for ongoing feedback, which can be used to make iterative adjustments to the strategy.

Creating an environment where team members feel valued and understood encourages open communication. This makes it easier to identify misalignments or practical hurdles that could derail change efforts. Addressing concerns often reduces resistance paving the way for more effective implementation and adaptation.

Engaging stakeholders at every level democratizes the change process and enriches it with diverse perspectives, resulting in more comprehensive and sustainable solutions. This inclusive approach eases transition while strengthening the organization, enhancing its resilience and ability to manage future changes more effectively.

Effective change management is about more than just enforcing new rules or processes, it's about transforming an organization in a way that is thoughtful, inclusive, and sustainable. By viewing resistance as a helpful guide rather than an adversary, you equip yourself with the tools to lead your organization through transformation successfully, ensuring a smoother transition and a stronger, more adaptable organization.

CHAPTER 6

Transparency in Turbulence: Communicating Through Change

How Does One Navigate the Storm of Change?

In the dim light of early morning, Susan stood by her office window, watching the city awaken beneath a blanket of fog. The sight was familiar, yet each morning brought a new shade to the scene. Today, it mirrored her thoughts — clouded and uncertain. She had been appointed as the new CEO of a mid-sized tech company grappling with declining morale and disjointed teams due to recent restructuring. Susan knew that her primary task was not only to steer the ship but to calm the waters.

She turned from the window and paced her office, her steps silent on the thick carpet. Her mind raced through conversations she had planned for today's meetings with department heads, informal chats by coffee machines, and addressing all hands in an attempt to clear the air. Each interaction was a thread in the larger tapestry of change she hoped to weave.

As she prepared for her day, memories of past leadership challenges flickered through her mind like old film reels. She remembered how open dialogues at her previous company had transformed an anxious workforce into an engaged one. The power of transparency wasn't just in revealing plans but in sharing reasons—the "WHY."

Mid-morning found Susan in a conference room filled with skeptical faces. She spoke earnestly about the changes, ensuring she addressed both what and why, linking them clearly to benefits for everyone involved. Her words were measured and clear; they needed to be both heard and felt.

Outside, a sudden shower pattered against the windows. Inside, as Susan concluded her talk, questions began to arise from the team — tough questions that made her realize this was just beginning.

Can open communication truly bridge gaps between present uncertainties and future aspirations?

Navigating the Storm: Why Clarity and Honesty Are Your Best Allies

Change is an inevitable force of any organization, yet it remains one of the most challenging endeavors to manage effectively. At the heart of successful change management lies the art of communication—clear, transparent, and timely. As leaders steer their organizations through transformative periods, the way they communicate can significantly dictate the outcome.

The essence of crafting a robust communication strategy is not merely relaying information but about constructing a narrative that resonates with every member of the organization. It's about articulating not just **what** is changing but **why** these changes are crucial and **how** they will impact everyone within the company. Such clarity does not just inform, it engages, persuades, and aligns diverse groups towards a common goal.

The Strategy Behind Transparency

A comprehensive communication strategy serves as your blueprint during organizational change. It ensures that every stakeholder understands the journey ahead, the reasons behind each decision, and their role in this collective venture. By addressing these elements, leaders can mitigate confusion and resistance which often arise from misinformation or lack of information.

Regular updates are another pillar of effective communication strategies. Change is a dynamic process; as such, communication must be ongoing to keep everyone informed and engaged. Regularly sharing updates not only reinforces the organization's commitment to transparency but also helps in adjusting strategies as feedback is received. This continuous loop of feedback and response is crucial for maintaining momentum and adapting to any unforeseen challenges that may arise.

Develop a Comprehensive Communication Strategy

Creating a comprehensive communication strategy is crucial in managing change effectively. It involves addressing the ***what***, but the ***why***, and ***how*** of the changes.

The **what** details the specific changes that are being implemented. It is essential for everyone in the organization to clearly understand what is changing, whether it is a shift in policy, the introduction of new technologies, or a restructuring of teams. The **how** involves the steps or processes that will be undertaken to achieve the desired changes. However, the most important aspect is the **why**—understanding the purpose and motivation behind the change. This clarity ensures that the message is not only delivered effectively but also resonates with the audience, driving meaningful and impactful change.

> A well-defined communication strategy ensures that everyone understands the changes, the reasons behind them, and how they will be impacted.

Enhance Team Alignment and Reduce Uncertainties

Regular updates are pivotal in enhancing team alignment and reducing uncertainties during times of change. Consistent communication can help in reinforcing the organization's commitment to transparency and can foster a culture of trust. When team members are regularly updated, they feel valued and integral to the transformation process.

Have you ever watched a relay race? The smooth exchange of the baton is crucial to maintaining the lead. In organizations, regular updates serve as this baton exchange, ensuring that every team member is on the same page and moving forward together without losing momentum.

Updates should not only communicate what has been accomplished but also what is forthcoming. This approach helps in setting clear expectations and preparing the team for upcoming tasks or changes. It is also beneficial to provide a forum for feedback, where employees can voice their concerns and suggestions.

Crafting Clarity: A Step-by-Step Guide to Effective Communication During Change

Navigating the complexities and uncertainties of change requires a well-structured and clear communication strategy. Here's how to implement one effectively:

Step 1: Identify Key Messages

Begin by pinpointing the essential information stakeholders need to know. Focus on the what, why, and how of the change. This clarity reduces confusion and aligns everyone's understanding and expectations. To create compelling key messages:

- **Align with Organizational Goals**: Ensure your messages reflect the broader mission, strategies, and objectives of your organization and your change initiative.
- **Use Brand Vocabulary**: Incorporate words and phrases that resonate with your organization's brand and with impacted audiences.

Step 2: Choose Appropriate Communication Channels

Select the most effective channels to reach your audience, whether through emails, meetings, or digital platforms. Tailoring the medium to your audience ensures that the message is received and understood. Consider the following:

- **Internal vs. External Channels**: Use internal channels like intranets, team meetings, coffee chats with leaders and internal social media for employees, and external channels like social media and press releases for broader audiences.
- **Channel Strengths**: Face-to-face meetings are effective for complex issues, while emails and digital platforms are suitable for detailed information.

Step 3: Create a Communication Plan

Outline when and how often communications will occur. This schedule should reflect the stages of the change process, ensuring stakeholders remain informed and engaged from start to finish. Key elements include:

Timeline and Milestones: Map out key dates and milestones to keep communication aligned with the change process.

Stakeholder Analysis: Identify who needs to be informed at each stage and tailor communication accordingly.

Identify Reviewer, Approvers, and Sender: Clearly define who will review, approve, and send each communication to ensure accountability and consistency.

Communication Frequency and Channels: Specify how often updates will be provided and through which channels (e.g., email, meetings, newsletters) to maintain regular and effective communication.

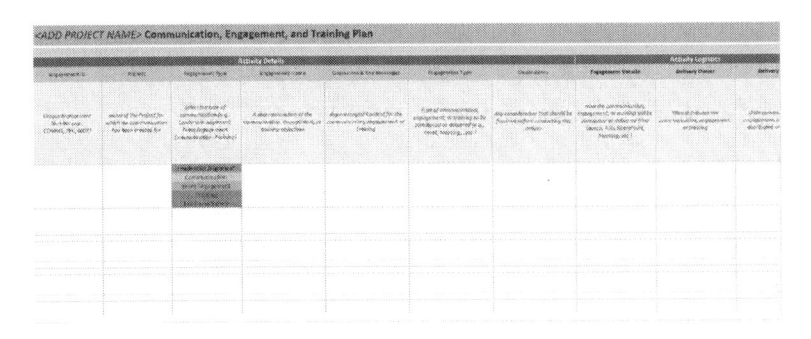

Figure 2: Pamela R. Fleming, (2024) Sample Communications Plan. Change Navigators LLC.

Step 4: Craft Clear and Consistent Messages

Use straightforward language and maintain consistency across all channels to build trust and credibility. Clear messaging prevents misunderstandings and establishes a strong foundation for change. Tips for crafting effective messages:

- **Clarity and Simplicity**: Avoid jargon and use simple language that is easy to understand.

- **Consistency**: Ensure all messages align with the overall communication strategy and are consistent across different channels.
- **Engagement**: Use storytelling and relatable examples to make messages more engaging.

Step 5: Encourage Two-Way Communication

Facilitate opportunities for feedback to foster an inclusive environment. This engagement is crucial for addressing concerns and adjusting strategies based on stakeholder input. Effective two-way communication involves:

- **Active Listening**: Pay attention to stakeholder feedback and show that their input is valued.
- **Feedback Loops**: Implement regular surveys, polls, and feedback sessions to gather insights and adjust strategies.
- **Transparency**: Be open about the change process and how feedback will be used to make improvements.

Step 6: Evaluate the Effectiveness of Communication

Regularly assess how well stakeholders understand and accept the changes. This feedback is vital for refining communication strategies and ensuring successful change implementation. Methods for evaluation include:

- **Metrics and KPIs**: Use specific metrics such as engagement rates, feedback scores, and message reach to measure effectiveness.
- **Surveys and Interviews**: Conduct surveys and interviews to gather qualitative data on stakeholder perceptions and understanding.
- **Continuous Improvement**: Use the evaluation results to make ongoing improvements to the communication strategy.

Step 7: Adjust the Communication Strategy as Needed

Be prepared to modify your approach based on feedback and changing circumstances. Flexibility is key to maintaining stakeholder trust and ensuring the initiative remains on track. Strategies for adjustment include:

- **Feedback Integration**: Regularly review feedback and make necessary adjustments to the communication plan.
- **Adaptive Messaging**: Tailor messages to different audience segments based on their needs and preferences.
- **Ongoing Training**: Provide training for communication teams to stay engaged and up to date on best practices and communication trends for effective communication.

Navigating periods of change requires steadfast commitment to transparency. By fostering open communication, leaders can build trust, alleviate uncertainties, and guide their teams with clarity and confidence. Embracing transparency not only strengthens organizational resilience but also empowers individuals to adapt and thrive amidst turbulence.

Let us remember that clear and honest communication is the cornerstone of effective change management, paving the way for a more cohesive and resilient future.

CHAPTER 7

Leading with Empathy: The Role of Emotional Intelligence

When Leadership Meets the Quiet Storm of Change

In the dim light of early morning, Michael sat at his desk, the soft hum of the computer blending with the distant calls of city life that drifted through his open window. Today, like many days recently, he found himself caught in a quiet storm—a storm of change that swirled around his company as it navigated a crucial transition. He was not just any participant; he was at the helm, responsible for guiding his team through this turbulence.

Michael leaned back in his chair; fingers laced behind his head. He remembered a conversation from years ago with a mentor who emphasized emotional intelligence and empathy as pillars for effective leadership. "People will forget what you said, but they will never forget how you made them feel," she had told him. Those words echoed in his mind now more than ever.

Outside, a gentle breeze stirred the early autumn leaves into a whispering dance. Michael watched them for a moment, their golden hues, a stark contrast to the grey undertones of the cityscape. It reminded him of the need for sensitivity to nuances—not only in nature but in human emotions too.

Back inside his office, he turned to face an array of photos on his wall: candid shots of team outings, laughter-filled meetings, and intense strategy sessions. Each image was a reminder of the bonds formed over shared goals and mutual respect—an emotional cache he needed to tap into now to steer his team effectively through these changing tides.

The phone rang suddenly, slicing through his trance—a call from Jennifer, one of his team leads who had been particularly affected by the restructuring. Her voice trembled slightly as she spoke about her fears and uncertainties. Michael listened intently, nodding even though she could not see him. Here was an opportunity not just to respond but to truly engage with empathy and understanding.

As they talked, Michael felt a shift within himself—a deeper

> recognition of the impact this change was having on individual lives within his team. It was not just about business strategies or outcomes; it was about people facing real fears and challenges.
>
> The conversation ended with promises of support and further discussions. Michael sat quietly for a few moments afterward, reflecting on how these individual interactions were critical touchpoints in leading through change.
>
> 💡 **Could it be that true leadership lies not only in guiding others but also in being open to learning from those that one leads?**

Why Emotional Intelligence is Your Ultimate Tool in Leading Change

Emotional intelligence (EI) and empathy are more than buzzwords; they are essential tools in the arsenal of any leader aiming to guide their organization through the challenging seas of change. As companies face the necessity to adapt or overhaul their structures and processes, the emotional landscape of their workforce can become fraught with uncertainty and resistance. It is here that EI becomes invaluable.

Leaders equipped with high levels of emotional intelligence are adept at navigating this landscape. They can **gauge the mood** of their organization, *understand unspoken concerns*, and address them in a manner that respects and validates the feelings of their employees.

The Impact of Emotional Intelligence on Change Leadership

Emotional intelligence (EI) serves as a cornerstone for effective leadership, especially during times of organizational change. Leaders with high EI can understand and manage their emotions, which in turn helps them navigate complex interpersonal dynamics sensitively and effectively. This ability is crucial when guiding a team through the uncertainties and stresses of change.

One way to visualize the impact of EI in leadership during change is to imagine it as a bridge. Just as a bridge helps people traverse over physical obstacles, emotional intelligence helps leaders' cross interpersonal divides and connect more deeply with their teams. It acts as a critical link between understanding and action, ensuring that decisions are made with a full appreciation of their emotional impact.

Research supports the effectiveness of emotionally intelligent leadership. Studies have shown that leaders who exhibit high emotional intelligence are better able to keep their teams motivated and cohesive during challenging times. This is because such leaders are proficient in recognizing and addressing the emotional needs and concerns of their employees, which fosters a supportive work environment.

Furthermore, emotionally intelligent leaders are adept at using empathy to foster trust and openness in their teams. By demonstrating understanding and concern for the feelings and challenges faced by their team members, leaders can build strong relationships that enhance team performance and resilience in the face of change.

Building an Empathetic Organizational Culture

Fostering a culture where empathy and support are viewed as integral elements of leadership can transform an organization. This section explores how leaders can model empathetic behaviors that encourage openness, collaboration, and mutual respect among all staff members. Such a culture boosts morale, productivity and loyalty–critical factors during periods of change.

By integrating emotional intelligence into their leadership style, leaders can ensure that change is not just managed but embraced as an opportunity for growth and innovation. This approach does not merely smooth out the bumps along the road, it paves a new road entirely towards organizational resilience and sustained success.

In embracing these practices, leaders do more than direct; they inspire and empower. EI is central in equipping those at the helm with the skills needed not just to steer through storms but to chart courses that others aspire to follow.

> **Emotional intelligence is essential for leaders to effectively guide their teams through transitions, ensuring decisions are empathetic and impactful.**

Techniques for Active Listening and Recognizing Emotional Cues

Active listening is more than just hearing words; it's about fully comprehending and engaging with the speaker on an emotional level. Leaders who master this skill are better equipped to understand the underlying concerns and motivations of their team members, which is vital during organizational changes.

A key aspect of active listening involves paying attention to non verbal cues such as body language and tone of voice. This requires a leader to be fully present and attentive, showing genuine interest and responding in ways that validate the speaker's feelings. This approach not only helps in gathering accurate information but also strengthens interpersonal relationships.

Rhetorical questions can be powerful in emphasizing the importance of emotional cues. How can a leader fully support their team if they are unaware of the team's fears and anxieties? Recognizing these emotional cues allows leaders to address concerns proactively, thereby maintaining morale and fostering a sense of security among team members.

To enhance their ability to listen actively, leaders can engage in exercises that focus on empathy and emotional responsiveness. Such practices might include role-playing scenarios that challenge leaders to respond solely based on emotional cues, thereby improving their sensitivity and responsiveness to such signals.

Using an analogy, consider active listening as tuning an instrument in an orchestra. Just as each instrument must be precisely tuned to contribute harmoniously to the ensemble, a leader must tune into the emotional frequencies of their team members to guide them effectively through the symphony of change.

> 💡 How might honing your active listening skills transform your effectiveness as a leader during change?

Incorporating empathy into leadership practices involves recognizing the personal and professional challenges that team members face during change and responding with support and understanding. This does not mean solving every problem for them, but providing a supportive environment where employees feel valued and understood.

Emotional Intelligence Leadership Model (EILM)

Daniel Goleman's Emotional Intelligence Leadership Model (EILM) is groundbreaking in the field of emotional intelligence. This innovative framework enhances leaders' ability to navigate the complexities of organizational change by leveraging emotional intelligence. Built on four pillars—Self-Awareness, Self-Management, Social Awareness, and Relationship Management—each element plays a crucial role in developing leaders who can effectively manage their own emotions and understand the emotions of others, fostering a supportive and productive work environment.

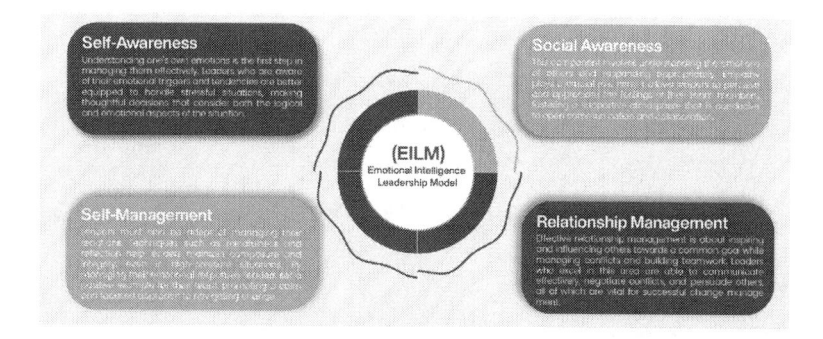

Figure 3: Adapted from Goleman, D., Boyatzis, R. & McKee, A. (2002). Primal Leadership: Realizing the Importance of Emotional Intelligence, Harvard. Business School Press: Boston.

Self-Awareness

Self-Awareness is the cornerstone of emotional intelligence. It entails a deep understanding of one's own emotions, identifying triggers, and recognizing how these emotions impact thoughts and behaviors. Leaders who possess high self-awareness are more adept at navigating stressful situations and making decisions that balance both rational and emotional considerations. This heightened self-awareness is crucial for effectively managing stress and making well-informed decisions, especially during times of organizational change.

Self-Awareness Techniques

To enhance your leadership effectiveness, consider incorporating the following self-awareness techniques into your personal development routine:

- **Regular Feedback**: Actively seeking feedback from peers, mentors, and team members offers valuable insights into how your actions and behaviors are perceived by others.
- **Journaling**: Maintaining a journal to reflect on daily experiences, emotions, and decisions can help leaders identify patterns and areas for improvement.

- **Self-Assessment Tools**: Utilizing tools such as personality assessments (e.g., Myers-Briggs, DISC) or emotional intelligence tests provides a structured approach to understanding your strengths and weaknesses.
- **Coaching and Mentorship**: Work with a coach or mentor for personalized guidance and support in developing self-awareness and enhancing leadership skills.
- **Reflective Practice**: Dedicating time to reflect on past experiences and decisions helps leaders understand their impact and learn from their actions.

> Self-awareness directly influences a leader's ability to manage stress and make informed decisions during organizational transitions.

Self-Management

Self-Management emphasizes the ability to control one's emotional reactions. Practicing mindfulness and reflection enable leaders to stay composed and uphold their integrity, even under intense pressure. By skillfully managing their emotions, leaders model a positive example for their team, fostering a calm and focused approach to handling change.

Self-Management Techniques

To enhance your ability to manage your emotions and behaviors effectively, consider incorporating the following self-management techniques into your daily routine:

- **Mindfulness and Meditation:** Engaging in mindfulness and meditation practices helps you remain present and manage stress effectively. These techniques enhance your ability to respond calmly to challenging situations.

- **Time Management:** Efficiently prioritizing tasks and managing your time ensures you stay on top of your responsibilities. Techniques such as the Pomodoro Technique or time blocking can be particularly beneficial.
- **Goal Setting:** Establishing clear, achievable goals provides direction and motivation. Breaking down larger goals into smaller, manageable tasks helps maintain steady progress.
- **Self-Reflection:** Regularly reflecting on your actions and decisions allows you to understand your strengths and identify areas for improvement. This can be achieved through journaling or taking time to contemplate your day.
- **Emotional Regulation:** Techniques like deep breathing, progressive muscle relaxation, and cognitive restructuring can effectively help you manage your emotions.
- **Healthy Lifestyle:** Maintaining a healthy lifestyle through regular exercise, a balanced diet, and adequate sleep supports your overall well-being and enhances your ability to manage stress.
- **Adaptability:** Being flexible and open to change enables you to adjust your strategies and approaches as needed, helping you stay resilient in the face of unexpected challenges.

Social Awareness

Social Awareness involves understanding and empathizing with the emotions of others. Empathy enables leaders to perceive and appreciate the feelings of their team members, fostering a supportive environment that encourages open communication and collaboration. This skill is essential for building strong relationships and ensuring that team members feel valued and understood.

Social Awareness Techniques

To further enhance social awareness, leaders can incorporate techniques such as active listening, empathetic acknowledgment, observing nonverbal cues, asking open-ended questions, being present and engaged, and understanding organizational culture.

- **Active Listening**: Truly listening to others without interrupting or planning your response ensures that you fully understand their perspectives and concerns.
- **Empathetic Acknowledgment**: Acknowledge and validate the emotions and experiences of others, demonstrating genuine care for their feelings.
- **Observing Nonverbal Cues**: Pay attention to body language, facial expressions, and tone of voice to gain deeper insights into how others are feeling.
- **Asking Open-Ended Questions**: Encourage open dialogue by asking questions that require more than a yes or no answer, allowing team members to express themselves more fully.
- **Being Present and Engaged**: Show genuine interest in conversations by maintaining eye contact, nodding, and providing feedback, which demonstrates full engagement.
- **Understanding Organizational Culture**: Be aware of the organization's values, norms, and dynamics to better understand the context in which your team operates.

Relationship Management

Relationship Management involves inspiring and influencing others towards a common goal while effectively managing conflicts and fostering teamwork. Leaders who excel in this area can communicate clearly, negotiate conflicts, and persuade others, all of which are essential for successful change management. Effective relationship management ensures that leaders can guide their teams through transitions smoothly and cohesively

Relationship Management Techniques

To enhance relationship management, leaders can integrate a variety of techniques into their daily routine, such as active listening, empathetic acknowledgment, observing nonverbal cues, asking open-ended questions, being present and engaged, understanding organizational culture, developing conflict resolution skills, and building trust.

- **Regular Check-ins**: Establish a routine of regular one-on-one check-ins with team members. These meetings should not only focus on projects or tasks but also on understanding their interests, career goals, and well-being.
- **Appreciation and Recognition**: Consistently recognize and celebrate the efforts and accomplishments of team members. Genuine recognition builds trust and rapport, fostering a positive work environment.
- **Transparency and Open Communication**: Create an environment where sharing ideas, concerns, and feedback is encouraged and valued. Transparency builds trust and strengthens relationships.
- **Building Shared Values**: Develop and promote a set of shared values within the team. This helps align everyone towards common goals and fosters a sense of unity and purpose.
- **Conflict Mediation**: Act as a mediator in conflicts, facilitating discussions to find mutually beneficial solutions. This approach ensures that conflicts are resolved constructively, and relationships are maintained.
- **Networking and Collaboration**: Encourage networking and collaboration both within and outside the organization. Building a broad network of relationships can provide new opportunities and insights.
- **Emotional Intelligence Development**: Invest in training and development programs focused on enhancing emotional intelligence. This helps leaders better understand and manage their own emotions and those of others.

- **Mentorship Programs**: Establish mentorship programs where experienced leaders can guide and support less experienced team members. This fosters a culture of continuous learning and development.

> The dynamic interaction between components of the EILM ensures leaders can effectively leverage emotional intelligence to lead organizational change, inspire commitment, and manage the complexities of transformation.

The techniques we've discussed here are far from theoretical; they are rooted in practical application and essential for monitoring organizational health and employee well-being during times of disruption. Leading with empathy transcends being just a leadership style; it is a strategic imperative that profoundly impacts an organization's resilience and overall success. By integrating these practices, leaders don't merely manage change—they cultivate an environment where change is embraced as a catalyst for growth and innovation.

As we delve deeper into the transformative power of effective change management, it's crucial to recognize that the journey, while complex, can be navigated successfully with the right emotional tools. This brings us to the Navi5ate Change Framework, a robust approach designed to empower leaders in steering their organizations through change with confidence and clarity.

In the next chapter, we will explore the Navi5ate Change Framework in detail, uncovering its five key components and how they can guide organizations toward enduring success and stability.

CHAPTER 8

Roadmap to Change: Orchestrating Change with the Navi5ate Change Framework

Can You Truly Predict the Future?

In the heart of downtown, where glass towers stretched to touch the sky and the streets buzzed with the ceaseless energy of commerce, Martin strolled through his usual lunchtime route. Today, however, his steps were burdened with a weightier contemplation than usual. As CEO of a burgeoning tech company, he had always prided himself on leading through foresight—anticipating trends that others overlooked. But recent shifts in technology and consumer behavior hinted at changes he had not foreseen, casting shadows of doubt over his future strategies.

The crisp autumn air brushed against Martin's face as he watched leaves dance their way to the ground—nature's own way of adapting to change. He thought about how trees shed their old leaves to make way for new growth. "Isn't this what I'm supposed to do with my company?" he pondered, feeling the parallel between nature's cycles and his business challenges.

Inside a small park bordered by aging brick buildings and newer constructions, Martin found an empty bench. He sat down, taking in the contrast around him—the old persisting alongside the new. It was here in this mixed scape of time where he often came to think. Today's dilemma involved integrating strategic foresight into his company's culture effectively. How could he ensure that every layer of his organization not only adapted to upcoming trends but also embraced these changes enthusiastically?

As children played nearby, their laughter piercing through his reverie intermittently, Martin recalled a seminar on strategic change management he had attended last year. The speaker emphasized the importance of embedding anticipatory skills within every team member, rather than simply the leadership circle. "Perhaps it's time for more radical internal shifts," Martin mused as a squirrel scampered near his feet, momentarily pulling him out from under his heavy thoughts.

His phone buzzed—a reminder from his assistant about an upcoming

> meeting with investors. They would be expecting not just forecasts but solid plans outlining how these forecasts would translate into actionable strategies. Martin knew that whatever decisions were made in today's boardroom would ripple far into the future.
>
> As he rose from the bench and headed back towards the towering inferno of industry and progress that housed his office, one question lingered in his mind: If we can learn from nature about cycles and renewal, can we also master its lesson on resilience against unforeseen forces?

Are You Ready to Lead Change or Be Led by It?

Staying ahead of the curve is non-negotiable for any organization striving for sustained success. Leaders who anticipate and adapt to emerging trends gain a decisive competitive edge. This insight is the backbone of the Navi5ate Change Framework—Change Navigator's proprietary methodology for executing change with unparalleled ease and precision.

Unlike one-size-fits-all approaches, the Navi5ate Change Framework is uniquely crafted to meet each client's specific needs. While it comprises five distinct phases, each strategy is tailored to the organization, ensuring a customized approach to change management.

Understanding the dynamics of change is crucial for any organization aiming for longevity and relevance. This framework empowers leaders to harness strategic foresight, enabling them to identify challenges and pivot their strategies in real time. By proactively adapting rather than reacting, organizations can not only survive but thrive in the face of uncertainty.

The Navi5ate Change Framework is built on five essential components, each addressing critical stages and facets of the change process. This structured approach equips leaders to manage transitions smoothly and confidently.

Moreover, fostering a culture of collaboration and empathy is essential. Acknowledging the human side of change management—recognizing the challenges and resistance that often arise—enhances the transition experience. This perspective not only facilitates smoother changes but also strengthens organizational culture, making it more resilient and adaptable.

By leveraging the Navi5ate Change Framework, leaders can deftly navigate the complexities of strategic change management, positioning their organizations for lasting success. Embrace this transformative approach to not just manage change, but to thrive in it.

Understanding the Navi5ate Change Framework

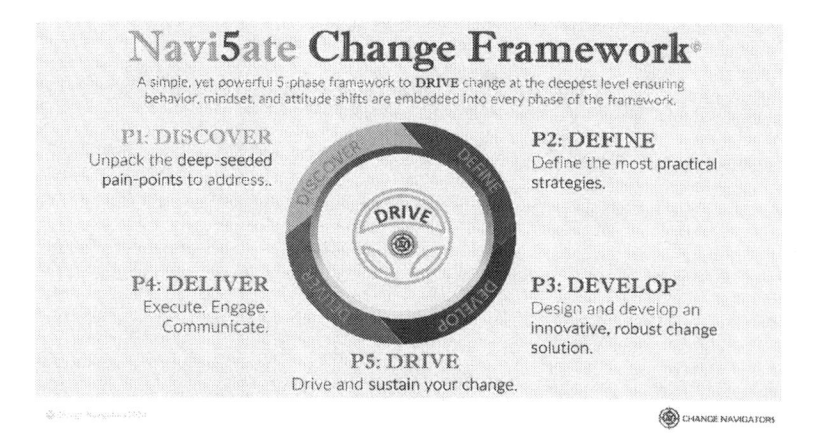

Figure 4: Pamela R. Fleming (2024) Change Navigators, Navi5ate Change Framework.

The **Navi5ate Change Framework** is Change Navigator's proprietary method for executing change with ease and precision. This framework is not a one-size-fits-all solution; instead, it is customized to meet the unique needs of each client. It consists of five essential phases: **Discover, Define, Develop, Deliver, and Drive**.

These phases form a continuous cycle that empowers businesses to initiate and sustain change effectively. Imagine navigating a ship through uncharted waters. The *Navi5ate Change Framework* serves as the navigational chart, where each stage marks a critical point in the journey.

1. The **Discover** stage, for instance, is like checking the ship's current position and condition before setting sail. It involves a thorough analysis of the organization's readiness for change, identifying potential obstacles, unearthing rocks, big and small, and understanding the overall landscape.
2. The **Define** stage ensures there is a clear and detailed map to follow. This includes defining and setting specific goals, timelines, and assigning roles, much like a captain outlines the route and delegates responsibilities to the crew. The define phase is crucial as it prepares the organization for expected (and unexpected) changes by developing customized strategies to address and mitigate risks.
3. The **Develop** stage ensures the right strategies and activities are developed based on data and insights from the previous phases, and that everyone is informed about the journey's progress. Regular updates, feedback mechanisms, and open lines of communication are akin to a ship's crew constantly interacting and updating each other about conditions and progress, prior to setting sail.
4. **Deliver**, the fourth stage, is where the actual journey begins. Here, the plans are put into action. This stage is about steering the ship, adjusting as needed based on real-time feedback, and monitoring the conditions encountered along the way. It emphasizes the importance of agility and the ability to respond to new challenges.
5. Finally, the **Drive** phase is where the change work hits the next level - sustainability. The Drive stage is about reflecting on the journey once the goal is achieved. It involves analyzing the outcomes, understanding what worked and what did not, and using these

insights to plan future endeavors. It also includes the tools for continuous monitoring and improvements post-change initiative. The Drive phase recognizes that once the goal is achieved, a new journey of sustainment and stabilization begins. Remember, change is a continuous journey, never a final destination.

6. If you are working alongside consultants, this is the phase where you take the reins and steer your change initiative forward. The role of consultants should remain as supportive passengers, guiding you until you feel fully equipped to navigate on your own. This approach ensures you develop both confidence and the skills necessary to sustain and enhance the changes independently.

The Navi5ate Change Framework underscores the significance of strategic foresight, empowering leaders to anticipate and adapt to emerging trends. By cultivating an atmosphere of collaboration and empathy, this approach thoughtfully addresses the human dimension of change management, acknowledging the challenges and resistance that frequently arise with new initiatives. This not only facilitates smoother transitions but also enhances organizational culture, fostering resilience and adaptability in the face of change.

> 💡 **How might viewing each phase of the "*Navi5ate Change framework*" as integral parts of a whole change the way we approach organizational transformation?**

Unleashing the Power of the Navi5ate Change Framework

Having highlighted the significance of each phase within the Navi5ate Change Framework, it is now imperative to delve into the specific strategies leaders can employ to drive change effectively. By harnessing these strategies, leaders can facilitate smooth transitions, cultivate engagement, and achieve sustainable growth within their organizations.

- **Discover: Map the Landscape**

  The Discover phase is all about gathering insights and understanding the current landscape before embarking on the change journey. During this phase, organizations conduct thorough assessments to identify the strengths, weaknesses, opportunities, and threats (SWOT) related to the change initiative.

  This involves collecting data through various methods such as surveys, interviews, focus groups, and benchmarking studies. The goal is to gain a comprehensive understanding of the current state, including existing processes, systems, and cultural dynamics that may impact the change.

  In addition to internal assessments, the Discover phase also involves exploring external factors that could influence the change. This includes analyzing market trends, competitive landscapes, and regulatory environments. By understanding both internal and external contexts, organizations can identify potential barriers and enablers of change. This phase is critical for building a solid foundation of knowledge that will inform the development of effective strategies and action plans in subsequent phases. It ensures that the change initiative is grounded in reality and tailored to the specific needs and circumstances of the organization.

- **Define: Align with Shared Goals**

  The Define phase is foundational, as it sets the stage for the entire change initiative. During this phase, the primary focus is on clearly defining and articulating the vision, objectives, and scope of the change. This involves identifying the key drivers for change, understanding the current state of the organization, and defining the desired future state. By establishing a clear and compelling vision, leaders can align the organization around a common goal and create a sense of urgency and purpose.

  In addition to defining the vision and objectives, this phase also involves identifying the stakeholders who will be impacted by the change and understanding their needs and concerns. This includes conducting initial high-level stakeholder analyses and mapping out their influence and interest in the change initiative. By engaging stakeholders early in the process, organizations can build support and address potential resistance. The Define phase is critical for laying a strong foundation for the change initiative, ensuring that everyone involved has a clear understanding of what the change entails and why it is necessary.

- **Develop: Build Inclusive Solutions**

    The Develop phase is crucial for building the necessary skills, knowledge, and capabilities within the organization to support the change initiative. During this phase, the focus is on creating and implementing training programs, workshops, and other educational activities that equip employees with the tools they need to adapt to new processes and technologies. This phase also involves developing support systems, such as mentoring and coaching, to ensure that employees have access to ongoing guidance and assistance as they navigate the change.

    Moreover, this phase includes **engagement activities** designed to involve employees actively in the change process. These activities can range from interactive workshops to feedback sessions, ensuring that employees feel heard and valued. Developing **comprehensive communications plans** is also a key component, as clear and consistent communication helps to align everyone with the change objectives and reduces uncertainty. Effective communication strategies ensure that all stakeholders are informed about the progress, benefits, and impacts of the change, fostering a sense of transparency and trust throughout the organization.

- **Deliver: Implement and Engage**

    Development is now complete, marking the next pivotal phase where strategies and activities are put into action. By leveraging collaborative tools, engagements, and training sessions that foster teamwork, we ensure stakeholders receive the right interventions at the right time and in the right manner. Ongoing stakeholder engagement and promoting knowledge-sharing across groups is essential. Using storytelling to celebrate shared achievements and cultural milestones reinforces unity and a sense of belonging within the organization. Recognizing and rewarding contributions and successes can motivate teams and sustain momentum.

This iterative process should be refined and executed with precision. Regular feedback loops and performance metrics should be established to monitor progress and make necessary adjustments. Engaging with key stakeholders through regular check-ins and updates ensures alignment and addresses any emerging concerns promptly.

- **Drive: Sustain and Evolve**

In this phase, leadership of the change process shifts to the client or the newly designated group responsible for advancing the change initiatives. You take on the primary role in driving these initiatives, while consultants provide support and guidance from the sidelines. Their purpose is to ensure you have the resources and confidence needed to navigate this journey independently. This approach empowers you to take ownership of the change, fostering a sense of responsibility and commitment to its success.

This is also where sustainability plans come into play. You will implement regular pulse checks and remediation activities, which should be carefully planned, executed, and monitored over a defined period post-implementation. This structured approach ensures that the changes made are not only maintained but also reinforced. These activities will help your organization transition back to Business as Usual (BAU) while preserving the improvements achieved through the change initiatives.

By adhering to this structured approach, you can ensure that the change is effectively implemented and sustained over the long term, resulting in a more resilient and adaptable organization.

Utilizing the Navi5ate Change Framework enables leaders to adeptly manage the complexities of organizational change. Through careful planning and execution across the Discover, Define, Develop, Deliver, and Drive phases, they can foster a culture of inclusivity, collaboration, and continuous improvement. This comprehensive approach not only addresses the diverse needs of the workforce but also ensures that the organization remains agile and resilient in the face of evolving challenges. By adopting these strategies, you will cultivate a cohesive and thriving organizational culture, well-prepared to adapt to future shifts.

Embracing Continuous Measurement in the Navi5ate Change Framework

Having explored the practical application of the Navi5ate Change framework, it is crucial to emphasize the importance of continuous measurement. This systematic approach not only facilitates the implementation of change but also enables organizations to assess its effectiveness and sustainability. Evaluating the impact of such a structured method is vital for understanding how change efforts translate into tangible outcomes and for optimizing future initiatives.

Staying agile and ready to pivot based on new information is essential. Continuous measurement allows organizations to adapt to evolving circumstances, make informed decisions, and drive sustainable growth. By focusing on measurement, leaders can ensure their change initiatives are not only successful but also resilient and adaptable in the face of new challenges.

Setting the Stage for Success in the Discover Phase

Discovery plays a key role in this process by providing the necessary insights to inform strategic decisions. By accurately assessing the current situation, leaders can define clear objectives, set relevant key performance indicators (KPIs), and develop targeted action plans. This ensures that the change efforts are data-driven, focused, and capable of delivering sustainable results. Here's how measurement plays a key role in the Discover phase:

Baseline Assessment:

Data Quality: Collect comprehensiveness and accurate data. Success is indicated by the extent to which the data provides a clear and detailed picture of the current state.

Gap Analysis: Evaluate the effectiveness of the gap analysis by assessing how well it identifies critical areas for improvement and aligns with organizational goals.

Data Collection Methods:

Surveys and Questionnaires: These tools help with collecting large amounts of data from employees, customers, and other stakeholders. They provide insights into perceptions, attitudes, and satisfaction levels.

Interviews and Focus Groups: These methods allow for deeper exploration of specific issues and provide qualitative data that can highlight underlying problems and opportunities.

Performance Metrics: Analyzing existing performance data to identify trends, strengths, and weaknesses.

Establishing Key Performance Indicators (KPIs):

Defining KPIs: Based on the initial diagnostics, relevant KPIs are established. These indicators will be used to measure progress and success throughout the change process.

Alignment with Objectives: Ensuring that the KPIs are aligned with the overall objectives of the change initiative. This alignment ensures that the measurements are meaningful and directly related to the desired outcomes.

Benchmarking:

Internal Benchmarking: Comparing current performance with past performance within the organization to identify trends and improvements.

External Benchmarking: Comparing the organization's performance with industry standards or competitors to understand relative positioning and identify best practices.

Continuous Monitoring and Feedback:

Real-Time Data Collection: Implementing systems to continuously collect data throughout the Discover phase. This allows for real-time monitoring and quick adjustments if needed.

Feedback Loops: Establishing mechanisms for regular feedback from stakeholders to ensure that the change initiative remains on track and addresses any emerging issues.

By prioritizing the foundational elements for project success, leaders can ensure that the Discover phase effectively establishes a solid groundwork for change initiatives. This strategy provides a clear roadmap for achieving desired outcomes, making certain that change efforts are data-driven, focused, and capable of delivering sustainable results.

Measurement in the Define Stage

The Define phase is crucial for transforming insights gained during the Discover phase into specific change initiatives and establishing clear, actionable goals. In this phase, organizations refine their objectives, create detailed action plans, and set metrics to monitor progress. Measurement is essential, as it ensures that these plans are realistic, aligned with strategic goals, and poised to achieve the desired outcomes. Here's how measurement is integrated into the Define phase:

Define KPIs:

Revisiting Initial KPIs: Define relevant and refined KPIs with the specific goals of this stage. Success is indicated by KPIs that accurately reflect the objectives and provide clear metrics for tracking progress.

SMART Goals: Evaluate the specificity, measurability, achievability, relevance, and time-bound nature of the goals. Success is indicated by goals that are well-defined and realistic.

Detailed Action Plans:

Milestones and Deliverables: Define a clear and feasible action plan, including defined milestones and deliverables. Success is indicated by well-structured plans that outline clear steps and timelines.

Responsibility Assignment: Assess the effectiveness of assigning responsibilities and defining performance measures. Success is indicated by clear accountability and measurable performance criteria.

Risk Assessment and Mitigation:

Identifying Risks: Define a through risk identification process. Success is indicated by a comprehensive list of potential risks and their impact on the change initiative.

Mitigation Plans: Define effectiveness mitigation plans. Success is indicated by well-developed plans that address identified risks and include metrics for monitoring their effectiveness.

Measurement in the Develop Stage

The Develop phase is vital for crafting the strategies, tools, and actions required to implement change initiatives effectively. During this phase, organizations convert their defined objectives into actionable plans and create the resources necessary to support these organizational initiatives.

Measurement is critical in this context, as it ensures that the strategies and tools are effective and aligned with overall goals. Here's how measurement is integrated into the Develop phase:

Action Plan Development:

Detailed Planning: Develop comprehensive change management action plans. Success is indicated by well-defined tasks, clear timelines, and assigned responsibilities that are realistic and achievable.

Resource Allocation: Evaluate the adequacy and efficiency of change resource allocation. Success is measured by the optimal use of time, budget, and personnel to support the action plans.

Tool Creation:

Developing Tools: Develop a customized set of tools to support the execution of strategies. Success is indicated by tools that are user-friendly, dependable, and tailored to specific change needs.

Customization: Assess the degree to which the tools are customized to meet specific requirements. Success is measured by the relevance and adaptability of the tools to the defined strategies.

Performance Metrics:

Tracking Progress: Develop a means to accurately and timely track the progress of change activities. Success is indicated by regular, accurate updates that reflect the true status of the change-related action plans.

Feedback Mechanisms: Develop an effective feedback mechanism to capture stakeholder input. Success is measured by the responsiveness and adaptability of the action plans based on feedback garnered from the tool.

Continuous Improvement:

Iterative Refinement: Measure the frequency and impact of refinements made to the tools and actions. Success is indicated by continuous improvements that enhance the effectiveness of the change initiative.

Readiness Assessment: Assess the organization's readiness to move to the next phase. Success is measured by the preparedness and confidence of the organization to implement the changes.

By emphasizing these measurement techniques, organizations can ensure that the Define and Develop phases effectively establish a strong foundation for successful change initiatives. This approach offers a clear, data-driven perspective of progress, facilitates timely adjustments, and ultimately leads to successful implementation.

Measuring Success in the Deliver Phase

The Deliver phase is crucial for ensuring that all parts of the organization are aligned and working together toward common goals. This phase focuses on the actual implementation of change initiatives, making accurate measurement of success essential for assessing alignment and effectiveness. Here's how to measure success in the Deliver phase:

Implementation of Change Initiatives:

Adherence to Plan: Measure how closely the implementation follows the defined action plans. Success is indicated by minimal deviations from the plan and timely completion of tasks.

Resource Utilization: Evaluate the efficiency of change resource use during implementation. Success is measured by optimal use of time, budget, and personnel without significant overruns.

Communication and Engagement:

Stakeholder Communication: Measure the effectiveness of communication strategies in keeping stakeholders informed and engaged.

Success is indicated by high levels of stakeholder awareness and understanding of the change initiatives.

Employee Engagement: Assess employee engagement levels through surveys and feedback. Success is measured by positive employee attitudes, high participation rates, and proactive involvement in the change process.

Training and Support:

Training Effectiveness: Measure the impact of training programs on employee skills and knowledge. Success is indicated by improved competency levels and the ability to apply new skills effectively.

Support Systems: Evaluate the availability and effectiveness of support systems (e.g., help desks, coaching). Success is measured by the timely resolution of issues and high satisfaction rates among employees.

Performance Monitoring:

KPI Tracking: Continuously track key performance indicators (KPIs) to measure progress towards the defined objectives. Success is indicated by positive trends in KPIs and the achievement of targets.

Real-Time Data Collection: Implement systems for real-time data collection to monitor ongoing performance. Success is measured by the accuracy and timeliness of data, enabling quick adjustments as needed.

Feedback and Adaptation:

Regular Feedback Loops: Establish regular feedback loops with stakeholders to gather insights and identify areas for improvement. Success is indicated by responsiveness to feedback and the ability to make timely adjustments.

Continuous Improvement: Measure the effectiveness of continuous improvement efforts. Success is indicated by iterative refinements that enhance the overall effectiveness of the change initiatives.

Alignment and Integration:

Organizational Alignment: Assess the alignment of various departments and teams with the change initiatives. Success is indicated by cohesive efforts and consistent messaging across the organization.

Integration of Changes: Measure how well the changes are integrated into daily operations. Success is indicated by seamless adoption of new processes and minimal disruption to business activities.

By prioritizing these measurement techniques, leaders can ensure that the Deliver phase effectively aligns every part of the organization with the change process. This approach provides a clear, data-driven view of progress, facilitates timely adjustments, and ultimately results in successful change implementation.

Measuring Success in the Drive Phase

The Drive phase is essential for evaluating outcomes against initial objectives and shaping future change initiatives. Typically occurring after implementation, this phase is where you begin to witness gains in adoption and utilization, as the organization transitions back to 'Business as Usual' (BAU). It's crucial to assess the depth of change capability embedded within the organization, as true change doesn't end with hypercare; this is where you measure long-term sustainability. Here's how to measure success in this final stage:

Outcome Analysis:

Comparing Results to Objectives: Measure the extent to which the outcomes align with the objectives set at the outset. Success is indicated by the achievement of the defined goals and targets.

Quantitative and Qualitative Analysis: Use both quantitative data (e.g., performance metrics, financial results) and qualitative insights (e.g., stakeholder feedback, employee satisfaction) to assess the overall impact of the change initiatives.

KPI Evaluation:

Final KPI Assessment: Evaluate the final key performance indicators (KPIs) to determine the success of the change initiatives. Success is indicated by positive trends and the achievement of KPI targets.

Trend Analysis: Analyze trends over time to understand the long-term impact of the changes. Success is measured by sustained improvements and stability in performance metrics.

Stakeholder Feedback:

Comprehensive Feedback Collection: Gather feedback from all relevant stakeholders, including employees, customers, and partners. Success is indicated by high levels of satisfaction and positive feedback regarding the change initiatives.

Feedback Integration: Measure the effectiveness of integrating stakeholder feedback into the final assessment. Success is indicated by the ability to address concerns and incorporate suggestions for future improvements.

Lessons Learned:

Identifying Successes and Challenges: Conduct a thorough review to identify what worked well and what challenges were encountered. Success is indicated by a clear understanding of the factors that contributed to success and those that need improvement.

Documenting Best Practices: Measure the effectiveness of documenting best practices and lessons learned. Success is indicated by comprehensive documentation that can be used to guide future change efforts.

Continuous Improvement:

Feedback Loop Completion: Ensure that the feedback loop is completed by using the insights gained to inform future change initiatives. Success is indicated by the implementation of improvements based on the lessons learned.

Ongoing Monitoring: Establish mechanisms for ongoing monitoring and continuous improvement. Success is measured by the organization's ability to adapt and refine its processes over time.

Sustainability:

Sustained Impact: Measure the sustainability of the changes implemented. Success is indicated by the long-term maintenance of improvements and the ability to build on the changes. Internal change capability building is critical to the success of sustainability.

Cultural Integration: Assess how well the changes have been integrated into the organizational culture. Success is indicated by widespread acceptance and adoption of new practices and behaviors.

By focusing on these measurement techniques, leaders can ensure that the Drive phase effectively analyzes outcomes, informs future change efforts, and completes the feedback loop necessary for continuous improvement. This approach provides a comprehensive understanding of the success of the change initiatives and sets the stage for ongoing development and refinement.

> The systematic approach of the *"Navi5ate Change Framework"* ensures that each step in the change process is purposeful and builds on the previous, leading to sustainable change.

By following these steps, leaders can effectively harness the Navi5ate Change Framework, guiding their organizations toward long-term success. Embracing this structured approach simplifies the complexities of change management while enhancing the potential for achieving outstanding results.

CHAPTER 9

Aligning the Alliance: Stakeholder Engagement Strategies

Can Data Illuminate the Path Through the Fog of Change?

In the soft glow of early morning, Thomas stood by the wide window of his office, overlooking the bustling city below. Today, like many days before, he found himself wrestling with the looming transformation his company was about to undergo. The board had decided it was time for a major shift in operational strategy to stay competitive. Thomas, head of strategic planning, felt the weight of this change on his shoulders as he watched the city stir to life.

The recent meetings were a blur of charts, projections, and heated discussions. Thomas remembered how data had been at both the heart and center of those discussions. *Data-driven decision-making,* he mused, turning from the window to his cluttered desk where reports and graphs lay scattered like leaves after a storm. He picked up a graph charting projected revenue growth. The crisp lines and sharp angles seemed reassuring—predictable outcomes based on solid data.

A sudden ring from his phone cut through his thoughts. It was Sarah, his lead data analyst. "We've run into some inconsistencies with the predictive models," she reported with a tone that managed to be both apologetic and urgent. As Thomas listened, he felt a familiar knot tighten in his stomach, the fear of unknown variables clouding their well-laid plans.

After hanging up, Thomas paced around his office. He stopped occasionally adjusting a frame or straightening a stack of papers, an unconscious attempt to impose order where he felt it was lacking internally. *Is relying on data truly enough to steer us through this upheaval?* he wondered silently. The question hung in the air like mist over a river at dawn.

He thought back to last year's initiative that failed despite favorable data predictions. The memory stung with fresh disappointment. Yet, there was also learning etched within those missteps; lessons about timing, market mood, unforeseen events—all elements that data had failed to capture fully.

Outside, the sun had climbed higher now, casting long shadows

> across gleaming skyscrapers and busy streets below. Inside Thomas' office, the sunlight reached across his desk illuminating dust motes dancing above an open report on change management strategies that highlighted continuous adjustment based on feedback loops—an ongoing cycle of action and reaction.
>
> Thomas sat down slowly in his desk chair as if settling into command at the helm of a ship entering uncertain waters guided only by stars and instruments alike—data in this metaphorical sense being both navigator and north star.

Harnessing Data to Master Change

In the realm of organizational transformation, the importance of data-driven decision-making cannot be overstated. Data serves as the backbone for effective stakeholder engagement, allowing leaders to make informed decisions that resonate with their teams and drive meaningful change. By leveraging data, organizations can identify trends, assess employee sentiment, and pinpoint areas that require immediate attention.

Real-time feedback mechanisms, such as surveys and analytics tools, empower leaders to understand how initiatives are being received at every level of the organization. Predictive analytics further enhance this capability by forecasting potential challenges and opportunities, enabling proactive adjustments to strategies before issues escalate.

Incorporating data into the change management process not only fosters a culture of transparency and accountability but also ensures that every move is calculated. When stakeholders see decisions grounded in solid data, their trust and buy-in increase, which is crucial for the success of any transformation effort. This strategic use of data ultimately enhances the likelihood of achieving desired outcomes and drives sustained organizational growth.

To maximize the impact of these efforts, organizations should harness the robust data gleaned from stakeholder mapping. By analyzing stakeholder interests, influences, and concerns, leaders can tailor their communication strategies and engagement efforts more effectively.

The Role of Data in Stakeholder Mapping

The first step in any successful change initiative is to thoroughly understand who the stakeholders are and what matters to them. This process goes beyond simply listing names and roles; it necessitates an in-depth exploration of their expectations, concerns, and the potential influence they wield over the project. Engaging with stakeholders at this level allows organizations to uncover invaluable insights that can shape the change process.

By leveraging data analytics, organizations can construct detailed stakeholder maps that not only identify each individual's position within the organizational ecosystem but also anticipate their likely reactions to proposed changes. This proactive approach enables leaders to tailor their communication strategies and engagement efforts, addressing specific fears and aligning stakeholder interests with the overall goals of the initiative.

Moreover, understanding stakeholder dynamics helps to foster an inclusive environment where individuals feel valued and empowered to contribute. By preemptively addressing concerns and demonstrating how change aligns with their interests, organizations can significantly reduce resistance. Ultimately, this thorough understanding of stakeholders paves the way for smoother implementation and increases the likelihood of achieving successful outcomes in the change initiative.

Key Benefits of Using Data in Stakeholder Mapping

- **Enhanced Accuracy:** Data-driven stakeholder mapping ensures that

the information is accurate and up to date, reducing the risk of overlooking critical stakeholders or misjudging their influence.
- **Predictive Insights:** Analytics can help predict how stakeholders might react to changes, allowing for better planning and communication strategies.
- **Tailored Engagement:** Understanding the specific needs and concerns of each stakeholder group enables more personalized and effective engagement strategies.
- **Risk Mitigation:** Identifying potential sources of resistance early on helps in developing strategies to mitigate these risks, ensuring smoother project execution.

Adaptability in Action

Executing a stakeholder assessment is not just important—it is essential. By truly understanding the voice of the customer, the change team can craft powerful strategies and engagement opportunities that resonate deeply with everyone involved.

Proactive leadership goes beyond merely navigating turbulent waters; it involves charting a compelling course that inspires others to follow. To maintain organizational relevance, leaders must anticipate future challenges while galvanizing their teams by aligning these challenges with overarching organizational goals. In this context, stakeholder engagement evolves from a mere tactical obligation into a strategic asset, fostering an environment where change is embraced and celebrated as a catalyst for innovation.

Organizational resilience emerges from this well-balanced interplay of foresight, adaptability, and visionary leadership. By grasping the human side of change management, leaders can forge deeper connections with their teams, facilitating smoother transitions and enhancing collective buy-in. This connection is strengthened through a thorough stakeholder assessment, ensuring that the strategies developed are not only robust but also inclusive and forward-thinking. In doing so, organizations position themselves not just to survive change, but to thrive in it.

<CHANGE INITIATIVE NAME> STAKEHOLDER ASSESSMENT							
Stakeholder Name/Group	Stakeholder Email	Stakeholder Location	Type of Stakeholder	Managerial Level of Stakeholder	Stakeholder's Influence Level (1=low - 10=High)	Expected Impact on this Stakeholder (1=low - 10=High)	Anticipated Level of Resistance to Change (1=low - 10=High)
Enter Stakeholder name	Email Address	Physocal Location	Business Unit	Senior Executives	1	1	1

Figure 5: Pamela R. Fleming (2024) Change Navigators, Sample Stakeholder Assessment Template.

Steps to Create a Data-Driven Stakeholder Map: A Strategic Blueprint

1. **Identify Stakeholders:** Using a stakeholder Assessment template, list all potential stakeholders, both internal and external, who might be affected by or have an influence on the project. This initial information will become the foundation of your mapping exercise for prioritizing stakeholders, guiding where to focus engagement efforts for maximum impact.
2. **Gather Data:** Collect data on each stakeholder's interests, influence, and potential impact on the project. A detailed stakeholder assessment is crucial. It helps in understanding not just the expectations but also the apprehensions and potential barriers posed by each group. This insight is invaluable in crafting engagement strategies that are both persuasive and respectful of each stakeholder's perspective.
3. **Analyze Data:** Use data analytics tools to analyze the collected data, identifying patterns and insights that can inform your stakeholder map.
4. **Create the Map:** Develop a visual representation of the stakeholders, categorizing them based on their level of influence and interest.

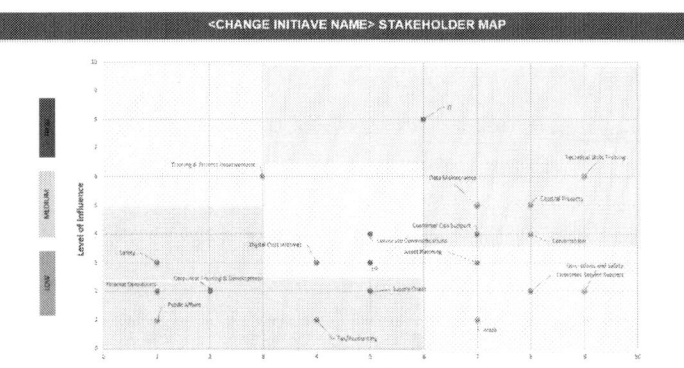

Figure 6: Pamela R. Fleming (2024) Change Navigators, Sample Stakeholder Mapping Template.

5. **Engage and Communicate:** With a clear understanding of who your stakeholders are and what they care about, you can craft a comprehensive engagement plan. This plan should outline the objectives, tactics, and timelines for engaging with each stakeholder group, utilizing the most effective communication channels and engagement methods.

6. **Adapt engagement strategies as needed:** Flexibility is key in stakeholder engagement. As you implement your strategies, continuous monitoring and feedback will highlight the need for adjustments. Stay responsive to this feedback, adapting your approach to better meet stakeholder needs and align with evolving organizational goals.

7. **Recognize and acknowledge stakeholders' "contributions":** Finally, acknowledging the contributions of stakeholders is crucial. Celebrating milestones and recognizing individual efforts not only bolsters morale but also reinforces the value of each stakeholder's investment in the change process.

This strategic approach to stakeholder engagement does much more than simply ease the transition during periods of change; it actively harnesses the collective insight, experience, and energy of everyone involved. By fostering an inclusive environment, organizations tap into a wealth of diverse perspectives and ideas, which enriches the change process and enhances problem-solving capabilities.

When stakeholders feel their voices are heard and valued, they are more likely to invest in the organization's evolving vision. This sense of ownership cultivates a deeper emotional commitment to the transformation, reinforcing a culture of collaboration and shared purpose. Moreover, such inclusivity not only smooths the immediate challenges of change but also lays a solid foundation for sustained success in the future. As stakeholders become champions of the change initiative, they help ensure that the organization remains agile and responsive, adapting to new challenges and opportunities as they arise. This holistic approach positions the organization for enduring growth and innovation long after the initial changes have been implemented.

> **Identifying stakeholders and analyzing their influence, impact, and expectations is essential for developing an effective engagement strategy tailored to their respective quadrants.**

Balancing Act: Meeting Diverse Needs

The complexity of change management often lies in balancing differing stakeholder needs without compromising the overarching goals of the organization. Data analytics offers a way out of this conundrum by providing a clear picture of potential conflicts and synergies between stakeholder groups. Armed with this information, leaders can devise strategies that harmonize these needs, fostering an environment where all voices are heard and valued. This not only mitigates conflict but also strengthens the collective resolve to achieve shared objectives.

Understanding the human aspect of change management involves recognizing the emotional journeys stakeholders undergo during transformations. Data-driven insights must therefore be complemented by an empathetic leadership approach that respects individual concerns while steering them towards a common vision.

Furthermore, collaboration emerges as a key theme in effective stakeholder engagement. By involving stakeholders in crafting solutions and decision-making processes, organizations can cultivate a sense of ownership among all parties involved. This collaborative spirit is essential for sustaining motivation and commitment throughout the change journey.

It is important to underscore the **impact** of these strategies on organizational resilience and ROI. Effective stakeholder engagement not only smoothens the path for transformation but also contributes to building a more agile and responsive organization. Through continuous evaluation, organizations can measure success not just by how well they executed the change but also by how these changes have positioned them for future challenges.

How can we ensure that every stakeholder not only hears about the changes but also understands and supports them? The answer lies in clear, consistent, and compelling communication tailored to the diverse audience that makes up an organization's stakeholder group.

> 💡 Could seeing things from stakeholders' perspective be the key to gaining their full support?

Effective engagement not only anticipates and mitigates resistance but fosters a collaborative environment conducive to successful change. By mapping out key stakeholders, developing tailored strategies, and balancing diverse needs, leaders can enhance support and foster informed decision-making throughout the change process.

CHAPTER 10

Decisions by Data: Empowering Change with Analytics

How Much Can One Bend Before They Break?

In the quiet corner of a bustling city office, Thomas sat, eyes closed, leaning back in his chair as the hum of computers and low murmurs of his colleagues filled the air. The scent of stale coffee lingered, mingling with the distant sound of traffic that seeped through the sealed windows. Today, like many before it, brought challenges that seemed to stack higher and higher, threatening to topple over.

Thomas opened his eyes and stared at the whiteboard across from him where the words "Resilience Training Session" were scrawled in bold. It was an initiative he had spearheaded, convinced that if his team could just weather the storm of relentless industry shifts and internal changes, they could emerge stronger. Yet doubt crept in like a persistent fog. Was he preparing them for success, or merely strapping them into a sinking ship?

He recalled last week's meeting where he had watched their faces, hopeful, yet shadowed with fatigue. The weight of uncertainty was etched deep into their furrowed brows. They looked to him for guidance, a captain navigating through uncharted waters.

A soft chime snapped Thomas back to reality; an email notification glowed on his screen. Another change in project direction — another test of their adaptability. He sighed deeply, rubbing his temples as he considered their options.

Outside, a cold breeze shook the trees lining the street below. Leaves fluttered wildly, clinging desperately before giving way to the wind's whims. Thomas watched them dance and fall; resilience in nature was not about standing firm but learning how to let go at the right moment.

He thought about his own role within this corporate ecosystem. Was he fostering growth or inadvertently pruning too harshly? As he pondered this balance between resilience and adaptability, he noticed Sarah from accounting approaching him with a hesitant step.

"Thomas," she began softly, almost drowned out by the sounds around them. "Do you think this new training will really make a

> difference?"
>
> Her question hung in the air like a delicate thread ready to snap under pressure.
>
> Thomas turned towards her with a gentle smile that masked his inner turmoil. "I believe it has to," he replied more confidently than he felt. "Without it, we might not bend when we need to but break instead."
>
> Sarah nodded slowly and walked away with a thoughtful expression that mirrored his own uncertainties.
>
> As Thomas watched her retreating figure merge with others in the office landscape—a tapestry weaving together threads of hope and doubt—he wondered silently if resilience was something one could truly teach or if it was something forged only through fire.
>
> Could they learn not just to survive change but to thrive within it?

Fostering a Culture of Data-Driven Decision Making

Having gathered valuable data and insights, the critical question becomes: What's next? The following step is to seamlessly integrate these insights into our decision-making processes. Fostering a culture of data-driven decision-making transcends mere access to data; it necessitates a fundamental shift in mindset across the entire organization. When decisions are consistently rooted in data, bias diminishes, and the likelihood of success increases. This cultural transformation ensures that every choice is made with a thorough understanding of its potential impact.

Imagine a ship navigating through foggy seas; in this metaphor, data acts as the lighthouse guiding it safely to shore. Just as a lighthouse illuminates the path to avoid perilous obstacles, data sheds light on the decision-making landscape, enabling organizations to make informed choices amidst the uncertainties of change.

To cultivate this culture, organizations must prioritize data literacy and provide employees with access to analytics tools. Empowering individuals at all levels to understand and utilize data reinforces the importance of evidence-based decisions and nurtures a more analytical approach to problem-solving. Regularly reviewing decision-making processes to ensure alignment with data-driven principles is also essential. This could include periodic training sessions, updates to analytics tools, and creating forums for employees to share insights and best practices.

Harnessing the transformative power of analytics is vital for guiding organizations through the complexities of change. Empowering change through analytics starts with a clear understanding of how data can forecast and assess the success of initiatives. By systematically analyzing outcomes, leaders can make informed decisions that not only align with organizational goals but also adapt to evolving circumstances. This predictive capability is instrumental in minimizing risks and maximizing the effectiveness of strategic interventions.

A robust feedback loop serves as a cornerstone for continuous improvement, ensuring that strategies remain relevant by integrating insights from all levels of the organization. This real-time feedback is vital for refining approaches, enhancing agility, and bolstering the organization's responsiveness.

Most importantly, nurturing a culture of data-driven decision-making is essential for sustained success. When every member of the organization engages in this analytical mindset, it fosters a collective resilience capable of weathering the challenges of change. This cultural shift is not merely about adopting new tools; it's about embracing a mindset that values evidence over intuition.

Integrating these elements not only improves the immediate outcomes of change initiatives but also builds a foundation for long-term resilience and adaptability. As organizations become more adept at leveraging data to inform their decisions, they enhance their capacity to navigate future uncertainties with confidence.

The journey through transformation may be complex, but with a data-driven approach, it becomes a navigable path leading to sustainable growth and enhanced operational efficiency. Thus, the role of analytics in change management transcends operational tasks; it is strategic, shaping the very core of how organizations adapt and thrive in the face of continuous change. By empowering teams with data, organizations enrich their understanding and engagement, turning challenges into opportunities for innovation and growth.

CHAPTER 11

Crafting the Core: Building Resilience and Adaptability

Can One Truly Capture the Essence of Time?

In the gentle embrace of dusk, Thomas walked through the park, each step crunching softly on the gravel path. His mind, a whirlpool of thoughts, fixated on his latest project: a novel about capturing moments that slip away before they can be fully appreciated. The cool air nipped at his cheeks as he pondered the elusive nature of time, much like trying to hold water in cupped hands.

He passed an old oak tree, its branches sprawling like the arms of an ancient sage. Children played nearby, their laughter piercing through the ambient sounds of the park — birds chirping, leaves rustling. Thomas watched them for a moment, their joy untainted by worries of the past or future. In their smiles and shrieks lay a secret perhaps — living fully in the now.

His sister had once told him about a photographer from another era who believed that capturing images could steal souls or trap moments forever. The thought lingered in his head as he sat on a worn bench overlooking a pond where ducks glided smoothly across their own reflections. Could he trap the essence in words as the photographer did with images? Could he stop time in its relentless march even for a brief moment within the pages of his book?

A jogger brushed past him, her footsteps rhythmic and determined, pulling him back to the present. He glanced at his watch — an hour had slipped by unnoticed. Time was mocking him again; always moving, never pausing for anyone to catch up.

As twilight deepened and stars began to prick the velvet sky, Thomas felt both challenged and inspired. Each person here seemed suspended in their own slice of eternity — some lost in conversation, some solitary like himself; all unaware that they were part of his silent study on time.

Could words ever capture what it means to live within these fleeting seconds?

Resilience Is Not Just Recovery; It is Your Strategic Advantage

As we delve into the penultimate discourse of our journey through transformative leadership and change management, it is crucial to hone in on perhaps the most pivotal assets an organization can cultivate resilience and adaptability. These are not merely buzzwords but are foundational elements that can determine the long-term success and sustainability of your company amidst continuous change.

The Bedrock of Sustained Success

Understanding and implementing resilience within an organization is not just about surviving turbulent times; it is about proactively cultivating a workforce that not only withstands change but thrives in the face of uncertainty. Resilience requires a strategic mindset that encourages adaptability and flexibility among employees, transforming challenges into opportunities for growth and innovation.

Fostering a culture that views change as an opportunity rather than a threat is essential for positioning organizations at the forefront of innovation and market leadership. This cultural shift involves training and empowering employees to embrace change, equipping them with the skills to navigate uncertainty with confidence. By encouraging a mindset that values experimentation and learning from failure, organizations can unleash the full potential of their teams.

Moreover, creating an environment where open communication and collaboration are prioritized allows for diverse perspectives to be shared, enhancing problem-solving capabilities. When employees feel supported and engaged, they are more likely to contribute innovative ideas that can lead to breakthrough solutions. This collaborative spirit not only strengthens the organization internally but also enhances its reputation externally, attracting top talent and fostering strong relationships with customers and stakeholders.

Ultimately, resilience becomes the bedrock of sustained success, enabling organizations to adapt to shifting market dynamics and customer needs. By embedding resilience into their culture, organizations ensure that they are not just reacting to change but actively shaping their futures, remaining agile and competitive in an ever-evolving landscape. This proactive approach not only secures immediate success but also lays the groundwork for long-term growth and sustainability.

Design and Implement Training Programs to Enhance Organizational Resilience

Organizations that thrive amidst change prioritize resilience as a core component of their strategy. Building this resilience begins with effective training programs that not only impart knowledge but also shape the attitudes and behaviors necessary for adaptability. By focusing on resilience, these training initiatives transcend mere skill acquisition; they cultivate an organizational culture that embraces change as an opportunity for growth.

To develop such programs, it is essential to identify the core areas most susceptible to disruption. Key focus areas might include change management, leadership development, employee experience, and communication skills. By tailoring training to reinforce these critical areas, organizations can prepare their teams for the specific challenges they may encounter. Incorporating real-world scenarios and case studies into the training helps employees not only to learn but to practice applying their skills in a safe environment, ensuring they are well-prepared for unexpected situations.

Moreover, effective training programs should foster a supportive learning environment that emphasizes continuous development. This can be achieved through ongoing learning opportunities, mentorship programs, and feedback mechanisms that encourage employees to grow and adapt over time. A culture of continuous improvement nurtures a proactive rather than reactive approach to challenges, allowing resilience to become a natural outcome of the organizational ethos.

Additionally, organizations should consider evaluating the effectiveness of their training programs through metrics such as employee engagement, retention rates, and overall performance in times of change. Regular assessments and updates to the training content can ensure that it remains relevant and effective in addressing emerging challenges.

Ultimately, by designing and implementing robust training programs focused on enhancing resilience, organizations not only equip their employees with the necessary skills to navigate change but also instill a sense of confidence and empowerment. This commitment to resilience fosters a more agile organization, better prepared to adapt to the dynamic business landscape and seize opportunities for innovation and growth.

Prepare Teams to Manage and Recover from Change-Induced Stresses

Change is often accompanied by stress, which can hinder an organization's progress and disrupt productivity. Preparing teams to effectively manage and recover from these stresses is vital for maintaining morale and ensuring continued performance. Understanding the dynamics of stress in the workplace is the first step toward addressing it effectively.

Teams that excel at managing stress exhibit common traits, including open communication, mutual support, and a clear understanding of their roles. By fostering these qualities through targeted training and team-building exercises, organizations can significantly alleviate the stress associated with change.

Imagine if every team member could view stress not as a barrier but as a challenge to overcome. This shift in perception is crucial for fostering resilience. Training programs that promote a growth mindset can transform stress from a source of anxiety into a catalyst for team development and innovation. By empowering teams to channel their stress into positive outcomes, organizations can enhance overall performance and cohesion.

Incorporating stress management techniques into daily routines further supports this effort. Practices such as mindfulness, regular communication forums, and wellness programs can help teams maintain focus and energy amid transitions. By embedding these practices into the organizational culture, teams become better equipped to handle the pressures of change, ultimately leading to a more resilient workforce.

The overarching theme of mastering effective change management has been woven throughout this discussion, underscoring the importance of a structured approach, empathetic leadership, and active stakeholder involvement. By applying the principles outlined in the Navi5ate Change framework, leaders can guide their organizations through transformation with minimal resistance and optimal outcomes. This proactive preparation not only equips teams to navigate change more effectively but also fosters a culture of resilience that contributes to long-term organizational success.

> 💡 **How might viewing stress as a manageable challenge change the way your teams operate?**

CHAPTER 12

Celebrating Small Wins: The Power of Acknowledging Milestones

Finding Your Way in a Sea of Change

Margaret stood by the large window in her office, watching the slow dance of autumn leaves as they spiraled to their resting places on the wet pavement below. The grey sky seemed to press down upon the city with a weight that mirrored her own feelings about the upcoming merger. Her company, a beacon in renewable energy, was joining forces with a larger conglomerate known for its ruthless efficiency but not for its care of employee spirits.

She turned from the window and glanced at the array of photos pinned to her bulletin board: pictures from team outings, award ceremonies, and holiday parties. Each snapshot captured moments of joy and camaraderie, milestones that had carried them through previous seasons of change. The thought surfaced gently at first - could celebrating these past achievements be the key to easing this new transition?

As she pondered this, her eyes caught sight of Tom setting up his desk for the day, arranging his little cactus plant and family photo just so. She remembered his skepticism when he first joined the team during last year's restructuring. It had been another minor celebration—a simple cake marking a project milestone—that had begun to shift his perspective.

The soft hum of conversation pulled her attention towards two colleagues discussing a technical problem by the coffee machine. Their laughter over some shared joke was a reminder of how shared moments—both big and small—wove a stronger fabric among team members.

Walking back to her desk, Margaret felt the cold from the glass seep through her blouse as she leaned against it once more. Could instilling regular recognition in their culture help them not just survive but thrive through this merger? Would celebrating both new and old milestones make them feel less like pawns in a corporate game and more like players shaping their future together?

The challenge loomed large but so did an opportunity—an

> opportunity to transform an organizational upheaval into a journey marked by victories worth celebrating. As she mulled over these thoughts, Margaret drafted an email proposing a new monthly celebration tradition aimed at highlighting individual and team achievements during this period of change.
>
> Could it be that in recognizing where they had been, they might better navigate where they were going?

Why Celebrating Milestones Could Be Your Most Powerful Change Management Tool

In an era where organizational transitions are both frequent and sometimes turbulent, it's essential to recognize that the way we manage these changes can profoundly impact our team's journey and the eventual outcomes. Celebrating small wins, often overlooked amid strategic realignments and operational adjustments, serves as a powerful tool in the change leader's toolkit. These celebrations not only bolster morale but also enhance employee engagement and, importantly, highlight the progress being made toward larger goals.

Acknowledging milestones during a transition period is crucial for several reasons. Psychologically, it creates a sense of achievement that fuels motivation and reinforces commitment to the change process. When teams see tangible evidence of progress, it fosters a culture of positivity and resilience, encouraging them to continue pushing forward even in challenging times.

Moreover, celebrating milestones helps to create a shared narrative around change, uniting team members in a common purpose. This sense of camaraderie can mitigate feelings of uncertainty and anxiety that often accompany transitions.

This chapter explores the psychological and motivational benefits of recognizing milestones, illustrating how these celebrations transcend mere feel-good moments and become strategic necessities. By embedding milestone celebrations into the change management process, leaders can harness their full potential to drive engagement and sustain momentum, ultimately leading to successful and lasting transformations. In doing so, organizations not only navigate change more effectively but also build a resilient workforce ready to embrace future challenges.

Understanding Psychological and Motivational Benefits

Celebrating milestones during periods of change is akin to watering plants in a flourishing garden. Just as water nourishes plants, enabling them to grow and thrive, recognizing achievements provides essential psychological nourishment to employees. This recognition boosts morale and motivates individuals to continue progressing, even when faced with significant challenges.

The psychological benefits of celebrating milestones are extensive. When teams acknowledge their achievements, it reinforces a positive mindset and mitigates the stress often associated with change. This affirmation of effort fosters a stronger emotional and psychological investment in their work, ultimately leading to increased job satisfaction and loyalty.

Consider a team engaged in a long-term project. The journey can be arduous, filled with unforeseen obstacles and setbacks. By celebrating both small wins and major milestones, the team can clearly see their progress, making the larger goals feel more attainable. This visible advancement acts as a powerful motivator, encouraging them to strive for the next set of objectives.

The motivational benefits of recognition are equally significant. Celebrations serve as psychological markers that confirm progress on the path to larger goals. They function not only as rewards but also as tools for setting future expectations. Employees feel energized and ready to tackle subsequent challenges, driven by the acknowledgment of their past efforts.

Moreover, celebrations tap into fundamental human needs for appreciation and belonging. When these needs are addressed, employees are more motivated to contribute actively to the team's objectives—especially during times of change when morale can be fragile and overall direction may be questioned. Recognizing milestones enhances a sense of collective achievement and unity among team members, fostering deeper connections within the organization and encouraging a more collaborative and supportive work environment.

The act of celebration not only acknowledges past achievements but also fuels the drive for future endeavors. It becomes a vital component in maintaining a motivated and psychologically healthy workforce amid transitions.

Implementing Recognition Strategies

So, how can organizations effectively recognize and celebrate achievements during times of transition? It begins with setting clear, attainable goals and communicating these transparently within the team. This clarity helps employees understand what specific accomplishments will be celebrated.

Employing a variety of recognition strategies can cater to the diverse personalities and roles within a team. Some individuals may appreciate public acknowledgment during meetings, while others might prefer a personal note or one-on-one conversation. Personalizing recognition to fit individual preferences is crucial for its effectiveness.

Combining formal and informal recognition strategies can also yield positive results. Formal methods might include awards or certificates, while informal strategies could be as simple as verbal praise or a team lunch. The key is to ensure that recognition is sincere and timely, reinforcing the value of the achievement.

Leveraging technology can streamline the process of tracking and celebrating milestones. Digital tools can help managers keep track of each team member's achievements and facilitate regular recognition, creating a constant feedback loop that is especially crucial during transitional periods.

Imagine a scenario where a team successfully overcomes a significant project hurdle. Celebrating this achievement immediately can reinforce positive behaviors and motivate the team to continue working toward the next milestone. It's about creating sustained momentum through positive reinforcement.

Building a Culture of Appreciation

Incorporating recognition into daily workflows can cultivate a vibrant culture of appreciation. This approach means not waiting for major successes to celebrate, but rather recognizing efforts and progress regularly. Such a culture boosts morale and encourages ongoing engagement and commitment to project goals.

Creating rituals around celebrations provides team members with something to anticipate. Whether it's a monthly gathering to acknowledge all achievements or special recognition during team meetings, these rituals can strengthen the team's cohesion and spirit.

Empowering employees to recognize their peers is another powerful strategy. Peer recognition can often be more impactful than acknowledgment from leadership, fostering a supportive environment that is critical during times of change.

It's important to remember that building a culture of appreciation is not a one-time effort but a continuous process. It requires commitment from all levels of the organization, particularly from leadership, who must model the behaviors they wish to see. By actively participating in celebrations and consistently recognizing team members' efforts, leaders set a standard that inspires others.

Together, these strategies not only address individual needs for recognition but also fortify the collective spirit essential for navigating transitions successfully. This approach has the potential to transform resistance into resilience.

Reinforcing Commitment and Boosting Morale

To reinforce commitment to change initiatives, integrating appreciation into the very fabric of the organizational culture is crucial. This ensures that recognition and celebration are viewed not as afterthoughts but as fundamental elements of the workplace environment.

Regular feedback sessions can be instrumental in this regard. They provide platforms for acknowledging accomplishments and discussing future goals, keeping everyone aligned and focused. Feedback should be constructive, encompassing recognition of efforts and achievements, thus serving as a comprehensive tool for motivation and improvement.

Leaders play a pivotal role in modeling the behaviors they wish to see. By actively engaging in celebrations and consistently recognizing their team's efforts, leaders reinforce the values of appreciation and recognition. This leadership behavior is contagious, setting a standard for the entire team.

Ultimately, fostering a culture of appreciation and collective effort leads to a more engaged and resilient workforce. It creates a supportive atmosphere that can endure and thrive during periods of change.

Incorporating recognition into everyday interactions, promoting peer appreciation, and ensuring ongoing commitment from leadership are essential components for nurturing a positive organizational culture. Together, these elements form a robust framework for supporting change initiatives and enhancing overall morale.

Celebrating milestones—both small and significant—is not just a feel-good activity but a strategic approach to managing and embracing change effectively. By acknowledging every step of progress, organizations can enhance morale, solidify team commitment, and facilitate smoother transitions.

Milestone Mapping

To effectively integrate this strategy, begin by defining what constitutes a "small win" within the scope of your ongoing change initiatives. Collaboration with team members is crucial to ensure that the milestones are relevant and recognized across the board.

Once these wins are defined, develop a communication plan that clearly informs everyone about these milestones and their significance. This could be through various channels such as emails, internal newsletters, or dedicated segments in team meetings.

Recognition should be timely and specific. Consider public shout-outs, visual displays of progress in common areas, or digital acknowledgments. These actions not only boost individual morale but also inspire others by setting a positive example.

It's vital to celebrate as a cohesive team. Organizing events or small gatherings allows everyone to reflect on the hurdles they have overcome together. Such activities strengthen the collective spirit and emphasize the shared journey of change.

Lastly, maintain an open feedback loop. Regularly solicit input on the recognition program itself and be prepared to adjust based on that feedback.

This responsiveness helps keep the program effective and appreciated, thereby continuously supporting high morale.

By fostering a culture that actively celebrates progress, leaders can boost morale and enhance organizational resilience. The emotional and psychological well-being of teams is crucial in navigating change successfully. Throughout this discussion, we have explored various dimensions of change management, emphasizing the need for empathy, understanding, and strategic action. Mapping milestones showcases the successes achieved through positive reinforcement, turning potential resistance into resilient, forward-moving momentum.

This approach is not only applicable to current changes but also serves as a valuable strategy for future transitions. As we embrace change, understanding and addressing the psychological impacts on our teams remains paramount. By celebrating small wins and major milestones alike, we ensure that our journey through change is not just endured but empowered, leading to sustainable success and a more engaged workforce.

Tying It All Together

As we approach the culmination of leading empathetically through periods of change, it becomes evident that managing transitions is not solely about reaching new operational states or achieving business outcomes. It is equally about how we get there—about the human journey through change. Celebrating small wins is pivotal in crafting a path that considers not just the what and the when, but also the who and the how.

By understanding and implementing these practices, leaders are better equipped to steer their teams through uncertainties with confidence and empathy. They turn potential resistance into resilience, paving the way for not just surviving change but thriving through it.

Our goal is to not only highlight effective strategies but also to inspire a reevaluation of how we view progress and success in times of change. In doing so, it connects deeply with every leader's mission: to guide their teams with foresight, strength, and above all, compassion. Through this lens, every small win celebrated is a step towards a more resilient and responsive organization—a true testament to leading with empathy in a world of relentless change.

What's Next...

Embracing the Journey: Transforming Challenges into Opportunities

As we conclude this exploration into the heart of effective change management, it is essential to recognize that the journey of transformation is both a challenge and a profound opportunity. The insights and strategies discussed are not merely theoretical but are grounded in real-world applications that can significantly impact your leadership and your organization.

The essence of this narrative is to guide you in understanding the nuanced dynamics of change through storytelling, how to leverage the Navi5ate Change Framework, and fostering an environment where every stakeholder feels valued and motivated. Throughout these pages, we have addressed the psychological barriers that often impede successful change and provided solutions to enhance both individual and organizational resilience.

Implementing these strategies goes beyond simply following a checklist; it demands a genuine commitment to empathetic leadership and an inclusive approach that values every voice within your organization. As leaders, you have a unique opportunity to leverage these insights to guide your teams through challenges and emerge even stronger on the other side.

Applying What You've Learned

To maximize the benefits of this book, think about how the principles outlined can be tailored to your unique context. Reflect on past change initiatives you've led or been a part of—identify what worked, what didn't, and how those outcomes could have been improved using the strategies discussed. Use these insights as a foundation for your future change efforts.

Start by engaging your team in open conversations about upcoming changes. Leverage the techniques from this book to create a customized transition plan that addresses both the logistical and human aspects of your initiatives. Remember, effective change management is an iterative process; continuously seek feedback and be ready to adapt as needed.

Additionally, reflect on the unique challenges and opportunities within your organization. How can the Navi5ate Change Framework be tailored to meet your specific needs? By cultivating an environment where every stakeholder feels valued and motivated, you can break down psychological barriers and strengthen both individual and organizational resilience. Let this book serve as your guide to navigating the complexities of change and achieving successful outcomes.

Acknowledging Limitations and Future Directions

No single book can fully encompass the complexities of change management. While we've explored various strategies and examples, there's still much to discover, especially in adapting the framework to diverse cultural contexts and emerging industries. This book is not merely about understanding tools and templates; it's about cultivating a change mindset and becoming a true change leader.

I urge you, as leaders, to contribute to this dynamic field by sharing your experiences and insights. Your real-world applications and feedback are vital in refining these concepts and making them more universally relevant. By doing so, you not only enhance your own leadership skills but also help shape the future of change management practices.

Embrace the journey of change with an open mind and a resilient spirit. The principles and strategies outlined here are just the beginning. Your commitment to continuous learning and adaptation will be the true measure of your success in leading transformative change.

Your Call to Action

Let this book ignite a fervent call to action! Challenge yourself to apply these concepts with intention and creativity in your organization. The journey of change may be fraught with uncertainties, but armed with the right tools and mindset, you can boldly lead your teams toward a future rich with growth and success.

Remember, transformation is not a one-time event; it's an ongoing process that requires a human-centric focus. Every step you take must acknowledge and empower the people involved. As you move forward, continually revisit the lessons learned here, refine your strategies, and strive for excellence in every endeavor.

> "The only way to make sense of change is to plunge into it, move with it, and join the dance." - Alan Watts

Change Leadership is a journey, and I urge you to embrace it wholeheartedly. May you find strength, resilience, and inspiration along the way, encouraging those around you to face change with courage and optimism. By cultivating a culture of continuous improvement and innovation, you can foster an environment where everyone thrives and actively contributes to a shared vision of success. Now is the time to act—your leadership can make a profound difference!

About Change Navigators

Change Navigators is a premier boutique change management consulting firm founded by Pamela Fleming, a seasoned expert with over 20 years of experience in the field. Pamela has held pivotal change management roles at renowned organizations such as PwC, Halliburton, and Memorial Hermann Health System, where she spearheaded numerous successful change enablement initiatives.

At Change Navigators, we specialize in guiding organizations through the complexities of change, fostering a culture of readiness and psychological safety. Our approach ensures that employees feel valued and included throughout transitions. We take pride in customizing our strategies to meet the unique needs of each client, emphasizing leadership development and strategic change management.

Service Offerings:

- **Leadership Development Programs:** Our Empowering the Core Leadership Development Program (ECORE-LDP) includes three tailored tracks for informal leaders, new and emerging leaders, and middle managers, all designed to enhance leadership capabilities and drive organizational success.
- **Technology Enablement Change (TEC) Hub™:** We integrate change management into technology-related implementations to improve awareness, understanding, and adoption. The TEC Hub also focuses on building Change Management Offices (CMOs), Change Centers of Excellence (CoEs), and Change Communities of Practice (CoPs).
- **Culture Connect Exchange (CCE) Program:** The (CCE) Program bridges foster a cohesive culture by integrating diverse perspectives. This three-month program, tailored to your organization's unique

structure, includes workshops and ongoing support to ensure every team member feels valued. Through assessments, employees gain insights into each other's perspectives and working styles, enhancing communication and collaboration. This builds stronger relationships, fosters mutual respect, and creates a more inclusive work environment, improving teamwork, higher employee satisfaction, and increased productivity.

- **Change Management Jumpstart:** The Change Management Jumpstart program is designed for organizations seeking initial guidance on implementing effective change initiatives. This eight to twelve-week program offers detailed assessments to understand your current state, foundational frameworks to build a solid change management strategy, and strategic recommendations tailored to your needs. Whether at the beginning of your change journey or looking to refine your approach, the Change Management Jumpstart program provides the tools and insights to help you move forward successfully and achieve your organizational goals.
- **Change Mastery Certification™**: A cost-effective Change Management certification program to equip individuals with the skills and knowledge to manage and lead change initiatives effectively.
- **Non-Change Practitioner Training:** Training program for employees who are not directly involved in change management but need to understand and support organizational change initiatives.

Navi5ate Change Framework

The **Navi5ate Change Framework** is a comprehensive flexible framework developed by Change Navigators LLC. This framework is designed to guide organizations through the complexities of change, and is adaptable, catering to the unique needs of each organization.

Why we Created This Framework

We created the Navi5ate Change Framework out of a deep passion for helping organizations navigate the complexities of change. This is not a "one-size-fits-all" approach. Successful change management goes beyond implementation; it requires ensuring that people transition effectively.

For further information on the concepts and tools discussed in the chapters, consulting or speaking engagement requests, or to contact Change Navigators LLC, please reach out to us at:

info@changenavigators-llc.com.

Visit our site at https://www.changenavigators-llc.com.

Reflections and Insights

Welcome to the Reflections and Insights section of our journey. This space is dedicated to your personal growth and leadership develop-ment. As you navigated through the chapters, you encountered thought-provoking questions, marked by a light bulb 💡 encouraging you to pause and reflect deeply.

Use this section to journal your thoughts, insights, and responses. This exercise is designed to help you internalize the concepts, challenge your perspectives, and truly engage with the material. By documenting your reflections, you create a valuable resource for your ongoing development, allowing you to track your progress and revisit your insights over time.

Reflecting on these prompts not only aids in understanding the material but also fosters a deeper connection with your leadership journey. It encourages you to think critically about your experiences, identify areas for improvement, and celebrate your growth. This process is essential for developing a well-rounded and effective leadership style.

Embrace this opportunity to grow, learn, and evolve into the leader you aspire to be.

Happy reflecting and may your leadership journey be transformative and enlightening!

Question: What steps might leaders take to effectively manage both emotional responses and organizational goals during change?

Question: Could the difference between a successful change and a failed one be as simple as ensuring that employees feel supported in their transitions? (Page 31)

Question: Could listening to employees' chorus of concerns not only ease the transition but improve it beyond what Thomas initially envisioned?
(Page 46)

Question: Can open communication truly bridge gaps between present uncertainties and future aspirations? (Page 56)

Question: Could it be that true leadership lies not only in guiding others but also in being open to learning from those that one leads? (Page 65)

Question: How might honing your active listening skills transform your effectiveness as a leader during change? (Page 68)

Question: How might viewing each phase of the "*Navi5ate Change Framework*" as integral parts of a whole change the way we approach organizational transformation? (Page 80)

Question: Could seeing things from stakeholders' perspective be the key to gaining their full support? (Page 103)

Question: How might viewing stress as a manageable challenge change the way your teams operate? (Page 114)

References

Bridges, W. and Bridges S. (2017, January 10). Managing Transitions (25th Anniversary Edition): Making the Most of Change. Balance Publisher.

Goleman, D., Boyatzis, R. & McKee, A. (2002). *Primal Leadership: Realizing the Importance of Emotional Intelligence*, Harvard. Business School Press: Boston.

Join The Collective. (2024, March 9). Emotional Intelligence Strategies for Managing Transformation Conflicts. https://www.jointhecollective.com/article/emotional-intelligence-a-key-driver-for-change-management/

Kulhari, R. Maslow's Hierarchy of Needs In Your Organization: How To Support Your Employees At Every Stage. Maslow's Hierarchy Of Needs In Your Organization: How To Support Your Employees At Every Stage

LaMarsh (2024). *Understanding Emotional Responses to Change: The Heart of Effective Change Management.* https://lamarsh.com/emotional-responses-to-change/

Landry, Lauren. (2019, April 3). *Why Emotional Intelligence Is Important in Leadership.* HBR Article: https://online.hbs.edu/blog/post/emotional-intelligence-in-leadership

MOC Solutions. (2024). Five Key Principles of Change Management. https://managementofchange.com/5-key-principles-of-change-management/

Presutti, L. (2020). *Healing Is Not Linear: Understanding the 5 Stages of Grief.* Healing Is Not Linear: Understanding the 5 Stages of Grief -

River Oaks Psychology

Drucker, Peter F. (2009). The Essential Drucker: The Best of Sixty Years of Peter Drucker's Essential Writings on Management. HarperCollins e-books.

William Bridges Associates. *Bridges Transition Model*. Retrieved from: https://wmbridges.com/about/whati-is-transition/

YouTube: (2014, May 5). Amy Edmondson – Building a Psychologically Safe Workplace. YouTube. https://youtu.be/BxC1Bl-4ZvE?si=wgbVfaCRAKI6N1wc

From Chaos to Clarity: Managing Change and Resistance delves into the complexities of organizational change, highlighting the critical role of effective change management. Through powerful storytelling, the book weaves together real-life examples and practical strategies to navigate and mitigate resistance, ensuring a smooth transition during technological and procedural organizational shifts. By focusing on the human element, it provides insights and tools to foster a culture of adaptability and resilience, ultimately transforming potential chaos into clarity and success.

ABOUT THE AUTHOR

Pamela Fleming is the Founder and CEO of Change Navigators, LLC, a boutique change management consulting firm. With over 20 years of experience, Pam has led successful global change initiatives across various industries, including Oil & Gas, Manufacturing, and Healthcare. Pamela is renowned for her expertise in organizational change management, helping companies navigate transitions smoothly and fostering inclusive leadership development.

Navigate Change, Embrace Success – Because Your Journey Deserves a Unique Path.

Pamela R. Fleming

Made in the USA
Columbia, SC
28 January 2025